WITNESS TO HISTORY

FROM VIENNA TO SHANGHAI: A MEMOIR OF ESCAPE, SURVIVAL AND RESILIENCE

Paul Hoffmann

Edited by
Jean Hoffmann Lewanda

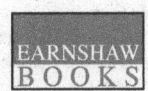

Witness to History

By Paul Hoffmann

Edited by Jean Hoffmann Lewanda

ISBN-13: 978-988-8552-74-0

© 2021 Paul Hoffmann

BIOGRAPHY & AUTOBIOGRAPHY

EB148

All rights reserved. No part of this book may be reproduced in material form, by any means, whether graphic, electronic, mechanical or other, including photocopying or information storage, in whole or in part. May not be used to prepare other publications without written permission from the publisher except in the case of brief quotations embodied in critical articles or reviews. For information contact sales@earnshawbooks.com

Published by Earnshaw Books Ltd. (Hong Kong)

In Memory of

My parents Paul and Shulamis Hoffmann
Two of the most courageous

and

My husband Doug Lewanda
Who taught me to be brave

Contents

FOREWORD by Jean Hoffmann Lewanda ... ix

INTRODUCTION ... xi
1. The Hoffmanns ... 1
2. The Singers ... 11
3. Oskar And Lili ... 19
4. Paul: The Early Years 1920–1932 ... 26
5. Storm Clouds Gather: 1934–1934 ... 35
6. Life Within Turmoil: 1935–1937 ... 43
7. 1938: The Worst Year ... 55
8. Leaving For Shanghai ... 66
9. Shanghai: Getting Settled ... 75
10. War Breaks Out ... 90
11. Pearl Harbor ... 99
12. The Ghetto: 1943–1945 ... 109
13. Peace: 1945–1946 ... 118
14. Young Shanghai Lawyer ... 124
15. The Communist Storm Gathers And Strikes: August 1948–August 1949 ... 137

16. Shirley — 145
17. Life Under The Communists: August 1950 – August 1952 — 154
18. Shanghai To New York: February 1952 – April 1953 — 165
19. The United States: The Early Years — 184
20. America The Beautiful: 1958 – 1998 — 196

EPILOGUE — 208
ACKNOWLEDGEMENTS — 272

Foreword

THE FOLLOWING STORY is my father's story. A father's story is never his alone. It belongs to all who love and know him. My father, Paul Hoffmann, intended this memoir to be a continuing chronicle of our family history. In its telling, it became a personal narrative of some of the most dramatic, intense and important events in world history. Born in Vienna, he moved to Shanghai in 1938 at the age of eighteen, and moved on from there to the United States in 1953. Dad was not only a reporter and observer of the events post-World War I, during World War II, and following the Communist take-over of China, he was a participant.

I cannot remember a time that I was not aware of my Austrian, Russian, Jewish, and Chinese heritage. Our home was decorated with beautiful carved Chinese furniture and tapestries. We consistently celebrated Jewish holidays every year. There was an endless parade of family and friends from all over the world, most of whom spoke English, but often reverted to the comfort of Russian and German when they came together with their landsmen. Our American neighbors often said they felt like they were at the United Nations when they crossed our threshold.

But there was more than the day-to-day exposure to a variety of cultures that influenced the young lives of my older brother, Abe, and me. There were the stories of life in Vienna and Shanghai and the subsequent flight from those former homelands, that were shared with the same frequency as the Exodus from Egypt at the Passover Seder. There was the constant awareness that we must stay vigilant to the events of the world. As a seven-year-old

WITNESS TO HISTORY

child, I vividly remember watching the trial of Adolf Eichmann on television with my father's commentary in the background. I can hear my father telling my mother to stock up on canned goods due to the uncertainty created by the Bay of Pigs Invasion. The implied message, even at an early age was: know who you are, be aware of what is happening around you and never assume that what is happening in the world is not your problem.

Dad began this memoir sometime after his retirement from his position as Trademark Counsel for General Electric Company in March 1986 and wrote his concluding comments in November 1998. Despite many years of challenges and struggle, he considered his to be a life well-lived and concluded with the wish that his children and grandchildren would also be able to say, "What a life I had!" After his passing in March of 2010, I not only rediscovered the manuscript of his memoir, but a wealth of documents and photographs covering over a hundred years of both family and world history, and the importance of his message was reignited.

It is in the memory of my father, Paul Hoffmann and my mother, Shulamis Froloff Hoffmann, and their wish that we be citizens of the world, that I share my father's story.

Jean Hoffmann Lewanda
May 2021

WITNESS TO HISTORY

1

THE HOFFMANNS

WHEN I WAS a boy of fifteen or sixteen years of age growing up in Vienna, Austria, a Hoffmann family chronicle surfaced. I was fascinated by it because it was in the form of anecdotes, rather than the usual enumeration of names, births, marriages, and death dates. Thus, I thought that I, in turn, should provide for my children and grandchildren a history of the family, particularly since I lived through some of the most turbulent times the world has ever known. The recollections of my grandparents and my own experiences cover more than one hundred and forty years, an amazing length of time, given the fantastic changes that have taken place in the world within that time span.

According to the chronicle, which disappeared with the dispersal of the family after 1938, the Hoffmanns lived in Frankfurt, Germany in the 1600s. Whether they came from Spain after the expulsion of the Jews from that country during the Inquisition is pure speculation. Why the Hoffmanns moved East around the year 1630 is also unknown. The first documented fact is that my great-grandfather Alexander Hoffmann, married Julie Knoepfelmacher (which means "button maker") in 1851 in the Hungarian village of Luky, now located in the Czech Republic, about fifty miles from Vienna.[1]

Two anecdotes from the chronicle are clearly fixed in my memory. One told the story of how one of my ancestors lent money to the Empress Maria Theresa of Austria to build the famous Schonbrunn Palace, the main summer residence of the Habsburg Family. That would place a Hoffmann ancestor in Vienna around the year 1750.

The other story was about an ancestor who came to Vienna to sell cattle in the 1850s. Having completed his transaction, he went to the coffee house, as was typical of the Viennese. He observed a card game, joined in, lost all the money he had earned from the sale of the cattle, and then decided to drown himself in the Danube.

Salomon and Jeanette Hoffmann

The story of our family started for me with the birth of my grandfather, Salomon Hoffmann, born on November 23, 1855 as the second child of Alexander and Julie Hoffmann. Alexander and Julie had six children. Their first two children, Israel and Judah, did not live past the age of two. Their four surviving children were one girl, Mindl, and three boys, Salomon, Isidor and Benjamin. Sometime after 1861, Alexander, who was a rabbi, moved his family to Vienna. I know very little about my Grandfather Salomon's youth or education. He told me he was in the Austrian army and described how the defenders of a city

---

[1] A family tree that traced the Knoepfelmachers back to Rabbi Judah Loewe, Chief Rabbi of Prague and Poland (1525-1609) was found in the early 2000's.

in the Balkans threw boiling pitch on the attackers. This was one of the many stories he told. Salomon married his cousin Jeanette Knoepfelmacher, around 1880. Jeanette's father, Jonas Knoepfelmacher, was also a rabbi.

I also don't know much about my grandfather's career. It was my understanding that he was the first custom peddler in Vienna. In any event, he was able to bring up seven children. My father, Oskar, fourth child of Salomon and Jeanette, told me that when he was a medical student he had to help his father by collecting weekly installments from customers. The reception from the customers when Father came to collect the installments was not always pleasant. Being Jewish did not help when one was asking for money. I never knew my Grandfather to work. I was told that when Grandfather was sixty years of age, he decided to retire and let his children support him. There was no social security in 1913. He was a lovable old gentleman and everyone liked him very much. He was a director of his synagogue, a rather large one, and I remember how proud he was to show off his grandchildren when they came to the synagogue on the High Holidays. I also remember being present when my Hoffmann grandparents celebrated their 50th wedding anniversary, a rare event in the early 1930s.[2]

Pazmaniten Synagogue 1935 – Gifted to Salomon Hoffmann on his 80th birthday

Grandfather came to our house nearly every day. He had a serious prostate condition, and my father took care of his medical needs.

---

2   The Pazmaniten Synagogue was one of the 267 synagogues destroyed on November 9, 1938, Kristalnacht

Operations were not as common in those days, and the risks were so much greater. Not infrequently, the phone would ring in the middle of the night. It would be Aunt Ilona, one of my father's older sisters who lived with my grandparents, to say that Grandfather was on his way to see my father to be catheterized. He would walk the fifteen minutes to our house in the middle of the night to minimize disturbing my father. It is interesting to note that there was no question of safety on the street, and no thought of taking a taxi. It was just too expensive and not necessary as long as one could walk. Grandfather died of prostate cancer in 1935 at the age of 81.

Grandmother Hoffmann, Jeanette, was a rather distant person. I never felt close to her and I doubt that any of the other grandchildren did either, with the exception of my cousin Franz who lived with my grandparents. His mother, Ilona, who we called Ila, had been widowed very young and never remarried. My grandmother suffered from depression. She took her own life in London by jumping from a window when she was about 80 years old. She had fled to England with her daughter Bertha, and her family, the Hohenbergs. Unfortunately, clinical depression runs in the family and a number of family members have in some cases suffered the devastating consequences of mental illness.

My best memories of the Hoffmann grandparents revolve around the first Seder night of Passover. The second Seder was celebrated with the Singer grandparents, a much more somber affair. Grandfather Hoffmann did a marvelous job of conducting the Seder and everybody sang and joked. Uncle Max, Bertha's husband, was the ringleader, always urging Grandfather to hurry through the prayers and rituals so that the matzoh balls would not get hard. Not all his jokes were quite so innocent. It was my job to recite the Manestaneh, the Four Questions, for several years since I was the youngest male.

PAUL HOFFMANN

My father, Oskar, had three brothers and three sisters. My Hoffmann grandparents clearly had their hands full with their four boys. Eduard was the oldest. While I did not know my Uncle Eduard very well, I heard about several of his exploits when he was young. There was the story of Eduard's army service around 1903. He had achieved the rank of lieutenant and had gotten drunk the night before his discharge. The next morning Eduard lined up his squad and told them that now that he was being discharged they all could "kiss his ass". As punishment for his behavior, he was not discharged and was thrown in the brig for a month. Although this event happened around the Jewish High Holidays, all the entreaties of Grandfather Hoffmann to get him released for the holidays did not help.

There was another story about how Eduard got himself into a brawl in a house of ill repute. My father, Oskar, was tasked with getting him out of jail. There was a trial and the doorman at the brothel was called as a witness. The timeframe around this event was Passover. When the doorman was asked his profession, he said that he was a matzah carrier delivering matzah for the holiday.

Later in life, Eduard suffered from multiple sclerosis and was in a wheelchair for as long as I can remember. He and his family were the only ones on Father's side who disappeared during the the Holocaust.

Uncle Eduard could not travel and his wife, Auguste, would, or could not, leave him. My parents offered to take their fifteen-year-old daughter, Jutta, with them to Shanghai at the end of 1939, but unfortunately my aunt could not bear to be separated from her daughter. Even at that late date, people did not grasp the seriousness of the situation. I shudder to think what the Nazis did to this beautiful girl

My uncle Friedrich, known to everyone as Fritz, was three

years younger than my father. He was a real charmer. Fritz was an executive at an insurance company and was very successful. Fritz's first adventure came when he was about two years old and he fell out of a third floor window. It was customary in Vienna to air the bedding on the windowsill every morning, something that was very necessary in a time and place where baths more than once a week were not customary. Little Fritz climbed on the bedding, the bedding shifted and he sailed out the window. Luckily, he landed in a tree and was not hurt, but the fright caused him to lose his speech. The story goes that he only regained it when Grandfather showed him the Austrian equivalent of a penny and he said "groschen". This affinity for money stayed with him throughout his life.

This was just one of many stories about Fritz. There was the story of how he was kicked out of school and never went back. Then there was the one about how he spent the whole of World War I in the hospital. He got there legitimately with dysentery, but from then on managed, with the help of my father, who was already practicing medicine, to fake one ailment after another. None of the Hoffmann boys was injured in the war, although they all served. Fritz married my mother's first cousin Amalia, known to all as Maltschi. Mother was very helpful in bringing the two together. She also had to absorb Maltschi's tantrums every time Fritz strayed. He was not only a ladies' man, he supposedly was a lady killer par excellence. The stories are innumerable and anyone who knew him cannot doubt that they are true. He had two children, Erich and Lotte. After Hitler came, Fritz's family first went to stay with Maltschi's relatives in Czechoslovakia. My mother's father, Grandfather Singer, was the only one of that branch of the family who had moved to Vienna. Fortunately, Fritz and family were able to keep a step ahead of the Nazis and came to the United States. Fritz was unable to rebuild a career in

Boston, but he and Maltschi kept their family afloat by running a boarding house. Fritz never seemed to lose his joie-de-vivre. He passed away in 1969 at age 78. Maltschi died in 1986 at age 88.

My Aunt Ilona, or Ila, was two years older than my father. She fell in love with a poor boy, Sigmund Kral, who by sheer hard work managed to become a doctor. He died of pneumonia shortly after their son Franz was born in 1909. As the story went, he literally worked himself to death, probably true then, compared to today when pneumonia rarely kills. Even though Ila was a very good-looking woman, she refused all offers of marriage. She devoted her life to her son, lived with her parents and also worked in the Hohenberg porcelain store. The family supported Ila and put Franz through medical school. When Hitler came, Franz, his wife Erna and Ila managed to escape to New Zealand. I had the pleasure of seeing Ila after the war here in the United States. At least she had a lot of pleasure from her three granddaughters, Dorothy, Susan and Marion, two of whom now live in Israel and one in Australia.

My Aunt Bertha, older than my father by four years, married Maxmilian Hohenberg. They had two sons, Kurt and Erich. Kurt studied law but had to work in the family porcelain store. He had to put aside his aspirations to be a lawyer when his father died in the mid 1930s. Erich was able to finish medical school in Vienna before 1938 and became the fifth doctor in the Hoffmann clan. The Hohenbergs all managed to emigrate to England. In 1941, Kurt and his wife moved to the United States. We remained close with him and his family, including his children John, Charlotte and Susan until Kurt died in 1973 at the age of 64. His mother, Aunt Bertha, met the same fate in London as her mother. She also took her own life by jumping from a window. She was only in her mid-fifties. Erich established himself as a well-liked doctor. I had the opportunity to visit with him and his wife Licci quite a bit on my frequent trips to London in the 1960s and 1970s. Unfortunately, he had inherited his father's high blood pressure and died in 1971 at the age of sixty.

There is a story about Erich to illustrate that soap operas imitate life and not the other way round. He had married Licci on the rebound and upon arriving in London met his old flame with predictable results. Licci worked in a book store and to help Erich, stole some medical books. When the theft came to light, he took all the blame and actually went to jail for a few months. While I know only the barest of facts about these events, it is not difficult to guess what was the impetus for Licci to steal the books, and then for Erich to accept the blame.

Richard was my father's youngest brother. Relations between the brothers were strained for as long as I can remember. Richard also studied medicine and graduated after World War I, probably around 1920. Father was doing very well at that time. He had opened his office as a specialist in skin and venereal diseases; the two specialties went together in Europe. Not surprisingly, there was a great deal of venereal disease after the First World War. Observing Father's success, Richard chose to specialize in dermatology as well. Richard then asked my father to join him in his practice. The negotiations failed, reportedly because Richard's demands were too high. Richard then opened his office very near Father's office. The two Dr. Hoffmanns having the same specialty with offices very close to each other lead to mistakes when patients were recommended to Dr. Hoffmann.

Richard's wife, Hella, was also a doctor, which may or may not have added to the confusion. I was told that Richard did profit from such mistakes and did not let patients know that they had reached the wrong Dr. Hoffmann. The situation was aggravated by the fact that within about ten years, Richard did better than Father. Richard certainly was the more energetic personality and aggressive of the two brothers. They did not talk to each other for years.

One incident illustrates the tension between the brothers. Father was a big wheel, a Grand Master, in the Freemasons. The Freemasons were a very select and rather small fraternity in Austria and other Central European countries, contrary to the rather open society in the Anglo-Saxon countries, particularly the United States. Richard wanted to be a Freemasons, but when he did not apply to my father's lodge, he was shunned on the basis that a man who does not want to be in a lodge with his own brother cannot be a "brother" to his fellow Masons. My father did not know about Richard's application and had nothing to do with his rejection, but Richard claimed that father had used his influence to bar him.

I will acknowledge that when I saw and heard of Richard and his family, both in Vienna and in the States, after World War II, relations were not improved between the two Dr. Hoffmann families. It must be admitted that because Richard was doing well financially he was very helpful to the Hoffmann grandparents and Aunt Ila in their later years. The way it worked was, whoever did better, carried the main burden; Father in the beginning, then Fritz and Richard later on. Richard and his family managed to migrate to the United States very soon after conditions began to deteriorate in Austria. The family had met the daughter of United States Secretary of the Treasury Henry Morgenthau during a vacation in Austria. She was able to get them visas very quickly and they left Vienna in 1938. Richard went to Boston where he became a very successful and wealthy dermatologist. To his credit, he tried to help the family as much as possible. He got Fritz and family out of Europe and he provided an affidavit to my sister Licci and her family enabling them to leave Shanghai in 1947. He paid one ticket for my parents' passage to Shanghai.

I believe he also provided the necessary documentation for my parents after the War that allowed them to come to the States. However, when my parents came to the States in 1951, Richard made it clear that he did not want them to settle in Boston. My sister had settled there, but did not advocate for our parents to settle in Boston. The more liberal admission policy for doctors in New York State may also have played a role in our parents settling in Upstate New York. Richard remained distant from the family, which may have been related to the difference in financial success that was felt by all concerned. His daughter Ruth's second marriage was to George Wald, a Nobel Prize winner. Richard's children, Ruth and Sasha, were the only two cousins of the twelve I never had any contact with.

There was one more thing about Richard. He was a lifelong Communist, an incongruous position to take by a person who was rich enough to garage his own car in Paris so that he would always have a car available on his yearly trips to Europe. As a matter of fact, he came to visit us in Italy in 1952. I distinctly remember how he explained to me, I who had barely escaped from Communist China, how marvelous Communism was and that I really did not understand the "glory" of Communism. I wish he could see that glory now. Richard died in the late 1960s and Hella passed in 1989, well into her nineties.

Finally, there was Stella, father's youngest sister. She was the same age as my mother and fifteen years younger than her oldest brother. She really was the baby in the family. She wanted to be a singer and had a nice voice, as did a number of the Hoffmanns, including my father, but by far not good enough for a professional career. As far as I know, she never worked. She married Rudolf Leitner. He was brought into the insurance company as an employee where Fritz was a director.

We were always very close with Aunt Stella and in the

summers spent almost every day with her at the beach on the Old Danube in Vienna. Stella and Rudolph and their daughters, Herta and Liesl, managed to escape to Israel by illegally crossing the border on a boat sailing down the Danube. After the war, they came to the States. Unfortunately, Stella soon contracted cancer and died in 1955 at only fifty seven years old. Rudolf died in 1990 at the age of ninety five. We remained in close contact with Liesl, who with her husband, Evgen, and their children, Peter and Ilana, moved to Connecticut and owned a delicatessen called the "Best Wurst". Herta and her husband Michael settled in Ohio before moving to New Hampshire to be close to their only son, Karl, and his family.

2

The Singers

My maternal grandfather, Maximilian Singer, was born on November 15, 1853 in Holice, a small town in what is now the Czech Republic, about a hundred miles from Vienna. His father, Ennoch Singer, was a farmer. The only thing I know about his mother was her maiden name was Geyduschek. My grandmother, Emilia Beer, was born on March 18, 1864, in Kremsier, Czechoslovakia. Her father, Marcus Max Baer was married to Charlotte Graetzer. The Baers were in the lingerie business. My Singer Grandparents were married in 1888.

I do not know why and when my Grandfather Singer came to Vienna, but I know for sure that he was in Vienna on December 8, 1881, the day of the great fire at the Ringtheater in which 447 people perished. He was attending a performance of The Tales of Hoffmann. He was on the fourth balcony and reportedly saved the lives of several people by helping them to jump out of a window, before saving himself by jumping

Lili's Parents

Newspaper article commemorating 50th anniversary of the Ringstrasse fire

into a net. We always celebrated Grandfather Singer's second birthday on December 8th. This episode emphasizes the rather accidental nature of life. Had he died in that fire, my mother clearly would not have been born. It boggles the mind to think of the consequences caused by the death of a single person.

Grandfather built a very successful wholesale business in ladies wear, primarily blouses, work dresses, aprons, and similar accessories. He applied to open a general store on February 9, 1903, at Salzgries 4 in Vienna and was given permission to do so one week later on February 16, 1903. In 1920, he was granted permission to manufacture textiles. The store remained at the same location until 1938, when the Nazis confiscated it, like all other Jewish property. The business eventually employed the whole family, except my mother, Lili, who was the youngest. I don't really know how my Grandfather Singer built his success, but he was a well-respected businessman. My guess is that he worked hard work, had solid business acumen, and my Grandmother was a great help. As a matter of fact, Mother told me that Grandmother ran her own little store at one time.

The relationships in the Singer family were in many ways the reverse of the Hoffmanns. In the Hoffmann family, the children took care of the parents in their old age. With the Singers, it was the grandparents who took care of everyone else. Father acted as my grandparent's physician, which required nearly daily visits. Father was paid for his services and this was certainly helpful during the Depression years. While Grandfather Hoffmann was well-liked, Grandfather Singer was well-respected. He was very taciturn. I hardly ever heard him say a word. True enough, from the time I was about ten years old, he was home, partially paralyzed from a stroke and in great pain, but I also have distinct memories of seeing him in his business, or at home, before the stroke and just cannot remember him ever saying much.

The role reversal continued with the grandmothers. It was Grandmother Singer who was close to all her grandchildren. She was interested in how we did in school and rewarded us when we did well. She gave us weekly pocket money and something extra on her and Grandfather's birthdays. While she was still involved in the business, when we visited we always got money for ice-cream in the summer and chestnuts in the winter. When both grandparents were confined to their apartment, it was the rule that the whole family went there every evening before dinner. Since it was customary to eat dinner only at 8 PM, it was possible for everyone to congregate at my grandparents' apartment after work, and most evenings I went along with my parents. It was only a fifteen-minute walk. There I saw all my uncles and aunts and most of my cousins. Obviously, there were the usual family quarrels and a lot of bickering, but the closeness of the whole family was certainly an important part of my youth and upbringing. Both grandparents were spared the horrors of Hitler. Grandfather died on June 10, 1935 in his eighty-first year after a final stroke. Grandmother who had heart trouble for a long time died on October 6, 1937. She was seventy four.

My mother's oldest sister, Stephanie, was eight years older than Mother. Mother told me Stephanie helped to raise her since Grandmother was active in the family business. Stephanie was a very good-looking but not a very happy woman. In her youth she had a bone disease, probably tuberculosis of the hip bone. In any event, she ended up with a limp because one leg was shortened in an operation. This handicap naturally influenced the rest of her life, particularly in a society where marriage was generally the only reasonable goal for a girl from a Jewish family. A husband had to be found; more difficult in those days because of her handicap. One of the clerks in the store, Arpad Merkado, liked her, maybe even fell in love with her, and needed little persuasion to marry into the Singer family. He had come to Vienna from Hungary, and while he was a very nice man, he was small in stature and did not have a formal education. I do not know what the financial arrangements were, but Uncle Arpad got some stake in the business. He struggled with an ambitious and sometimes frustrated wife. Things were certainly aggravated by the death of their older son, Hans, who died at the age of eleven from heart disease, a valve problem, quite easily fixed these days. Steffi wanted to be a singer, but did not possess the level of talent necessary to pursue a career. Hans played the violin and supposedly was very good. This may explain his younger brother Fred's desire to have his daughter, named Stephanie for her grandmother, to be a musician. When Hitler came, Fred was sent to live with his father's cousin in Washington. He was only fifteen. Fred ran away from his uncle to some friends in New York because he was being mistreated by his uncle. Fred enlisted and served in the Pacific theater, surviving a serious head injury. Fred's parents held out waiting for visas to go to the States to join their only son. We probably could have gotten them to Shanghai. The United States visas did not arrive in time and they disappeared in the Holocaust. Once again, like in the case of Eduard Hoffmann, parental considerations overshadowed the reality of the danger.

Aunt Margit was six years older than Mother and her second oldest sister. She married an engineer, Siegmund Katscher, known as Sigi. Margit was pregnant when she married Sigi. Their first child, Kurt, died at the age of three or four. The story was that Sigi had syphilis and the child contracted the disease and died from it. Eventually, both Sigi and Margit were cured and had two more children, Lotte and Kathe. Sigi was a very well-known stamp collector in Vienna, and got me started collecting stamps. I actually took a nice little collection to Shanghai, which today probably would be worth a lot of money, but I had to sell it during the War. Sigi had something to do with the invention or improvement of records. I only know that my Grandfather Singer invested in the invention and lost money when something went wrong with the patents.

Sigi never seemed to have a fixed job, concentrating mostly on his stamps. Margit had to work in the family business and I understand she was very good at what she did. Sigi died in the mid-1930s of a kidney problem. Margit later married a bachelor cousin, Dr. Edmund Blau-Haas, sometime after arriving in Shanghai. The two girls, who were known as Lotte and Kitty, were an interesting study in contrasts, and remained so all their lives. Lotte was very pretty, very flighty, and always a problem to her widowed mother, who simply could not handle her. Kitty, in contrast, was very serious, very ambitious and by far the best student among all the Singer grandchildren. She was always held up as an example to the rest of us.

After Hitler came, Lotte married against the wishes of both sets of parents. She and her husband crossed the border illegally and eventually got to France where they became separated during the War. Her husband disappeared. Lotte ended up in a concentration camp in Belgium, where she met, and then later married, her second husband, Bernard. Kitty was only fifteen in 1938 and was sent to England on the Kindertransport, a children's rescue operation. After some very difficult times, she served in the British army, married an Englishman, raised her daughter, Jackie, and became an elementary school teacher in England. I managed to get landing permits to Shanghai for Margit and Edmund and they spent the war years with us there. After the War, they went to England to join Kitty where they both passed away. Margit was only sixty-three years old.

Ernst was the third child and the older son. As was customary, he was expected to go into the family business, which he did. He was the heir-apparent, a continuous source of annoyance for Steffi, who wanted her husband to be more assertive and more of an equal in the business. I believe Ernst became the principal owner after grandfather died. He married a young apprentice in the store, Toni, supposedly against the wishes of his parents. Toni was not considered to be of the right social class. Toni continued to work in the store after their marriage. It was way easier for women in those days to work because all middle class families had maids.

It is not difficult to visualize all the problems created by so many close family members working in the same establishment. My grandfather and the two men, Ernst and Arpad, were responsible for dealing with customers and managing the store.

Grandmother Singer, Margit and Toni dealt with design and production. Grandfather Singer must have been quite a man to keep them all working together and the business operating smoothly. Despite the strains, the family members always talked to each other.

Ernst and Toni had two children, Trude and Felix. I remember Uncle Ernst joked a lot. He also liked to drink, and Father and he would match cognacs most evenings at my grandparent's house. No one ever talked about father drinking too much, but there was talk that Ernst did. In retrospect, there was some truth to this. Soon after the Nazis took over, Ernst was arrested. I don't know under what pretext, but the pretext couldn't have been too serious because he was released fairly quickly. Ernst and family left as soon as possible thereafter for Czechoslovakia to be with my mother's side of the family. From there, they were able to get to the United States. The Jewish Joint Distribution Committee decided to settle them in Mobile, Alabama, where Ernst worked as an accountant. He died very young at only fifty-two years of age in 1946. Most of the men in Grandmother Singer's family died young from heart disease.

Unfortunately, mother explained this to me when I was maybe ten or eleven years old and it left a deep impression on me. For a long time, I believed I was going to die young like they did. I obviously know better today, but paid a price for my beliefs and my mother's poor understanding of psychology. How many parents say things in a well-meaning, yet thoughtless, way without realizing how deeply they influence their children's lives? Trude married twice, having lost her first husband very early in the War. He disappeared with his plane over the Gulf of Mexico. She settled in Pearson, Georgia. Felix developed mental health problems. We saw him once in New York in 1954, but he seemed to weave in and out of the family scene.³

Mother's younger brother was Jacques, two years older than she. He was slated to be a doctor. All Jewish families aspired to have at least one medical doctor in the family. When the First World War, the Great War, broke out, he was a tall, thin eighteen-year-old kid. He was very patriotic and anxious to join the army and fight for the Kaiser and the Fatherland. He literally fattened himself up to be able to enlist. He succeeded, and in 1917, two months before my parents' wedding, he took shrapnel to the groin on the Italian front. The story was that he didn't let himself be helped since others were more seriously injured. Infection set in and he died from a wound that he would have certainly survived in today's world. I was told about the reaction of Grandfather Singer to the tragedy, and I believe it since it was totally in character. All Grandfather said about the loss of his favorite son, as he went to pray at the little synagogue that he frequented, and reputedly supported single-handedly, was "God gives and God takes."

---

3   Felix passed away in Denver, Colorado in 2007. He was a writer and was arrested while protesting during the Civil Rights Era. His arrest photo can be seen in the Mississippi Civil Rights Archive circa 1961.

3

OSKAR AND LILI

MY FATHER, Oskar, was born on March 12, 1888. To appreciate how long ago this was, electric lighting had just been invented, but there certainly was none in Vienna. There was no telephone, no radio, and no modern medicine. Johann Strauss was in his heyday and Father may even have seen him conduct the orchestra in Vienna. While I was very close to Father, we never talked about his early childhood. His stories started with his last year in the gymnasium, the equivalent of being a senior in high school. He told me how he cut so many classes to take girls to the park that he failed his Latin course. Father had to take a make-up exam after the summer so that he could enter the University. The apple doesn't fall far from the tree since I had my difficulties in my junior year in high school for similar reasons.

Father was expected to be a rabbi, but did not choose this vocation. Instead, in the fall of 1906, he started his medical studies at Vienna University, which in those days was one of the premier universities in the world. Everyone who had graduated from the gymnasium, as high-school is still called in Vienna, was admitted. The selection process took place during the eight years of gymnasium. However, for Jews there were restrictions, officially and unofficially. Only a certain number were to be admitted each year. I do not know why Father was among that chosen group. He must have been a good student because it was difficult to pass all the examinations. All examinations were oral and thus the whim and mood of the professor were a factor. If you failed, you could repeat the exam twice, and after that you were out of luck. It didn't help to be Jewish, unless the professor was Jewish, like the great Julius Tandler, the authority of his time in anatomy. Sigmund Freud, the Father of Modern Psychiatry, also taught in Vienna during this era.

Two episodes of Father's student days have stuck in my mind, both having to do with his political views and quick temper, which was not uncharacteristic of him. One happened during a political demonstration. He was watching the demonstration and was told to move on by a policeman. He refused, insisting on his right to stand anywhere he liked. He was right, but the policeman didn't think so and arrested him. Grandfather Hoffmann insisted that he would let Father go to jail, but when the police came to take him, Grandfather decided to pay the fine.

Another time, Father passed the University in a trolley car and saw that Jewish students were being beaten. I never understood how he was able to decide what was happening; maybe he heard the epithets being shouted. Father jumped off the trolley to join the fracas and came home with a bloody head. This character trait of standing up for his rights and his opposition to political oppression will reappear several times during the telling of this story.

Father received his doctorate in 1911 and decided to specialize in dermatology, which in those days also included venereal diseases. I don't know what made him choose this specialty. Could it be that it was one that very rarely dealt with emergencies and even more rarely led to calls at night? He started his internship at the Wiener Krankenhaus (Hospital) where he stayed until he was drafted into the army at the height of World

War I. According to Father, he had a falling out with his superior at the hospital, who told him to conform and buckle down or get sent to the War. True to form, Father refused and promptly was shipped out. Father claimed that he had to leave Vienna anyway, to get away from the girls. The War had obviously led to a great shortage of men and a twenty-eight-year-old doctor had his hands full. Father also had developed some lung trouble and the outdoor life in the Carpathian Mountains of Romania was very healthy. Father claimed the War saved his life. The War really did save his life when the Nazis took over Austria. He had earned a couple of medals, which he said were undeserved, but those medals influenced the Nazis to grant a delay in the deportation to Poland of my parents in 1939, permitting them enough time to leave for Shanghai.

One of the medals was earned when Father and his unit got lost and, as he told it, spent a very good week between the lines. He generally kept the bloody aspects of the war to himself. As a doctor, Father must have seen some terrible horrors. He only mentioned how he had to work around the clock sometimes, and once was so exhausted that he slept for twenty-four hours, right through a bombardment.

On one of his leaves, he met Mother.

Mother was born on December 7, 1898. She also did not speak too much about her youth. Maybe this was because there wasn't too much youth to speak of. She was not yet sixteen when the War broke out and married before she was nineteen. Both of Mother's parents worked and the maid took care of the children. Steffi, eight years Mother's senior, acted as a substitute mother. The Singers were well-to-do and mother said that she had a pleasant childhood. One of her memories was the sixtieth anniversary of the reign of Emperor Franz Joseph and the festivities accompanying the Diamond Jubilee in 1908, including the arrival of electric street lighting in Vienna and the opening of one of the show pieces of the city, the Ringstrasse, with its beautiful buildings.

Mother often mentioned that as a young woman, she would say that money is not important, because if you have it, it does not matter and if you do not, it cannot matter. How, later on, she became such a compulsive worrier, particularly about money, does not square with this motto. She said that her attitude towards money was not rooted in her childhood, so one can only guess that it was an inherited trait, aggravated by the Depression and emigration. Looking at my own attitude on the subject, I am sure that there is an inherited factor, plus acquired insecurities.

One subject Mother often spoke about was her desire to study, but my Grandfather Singer did not believe in girls going beyond eighth grade, the end of compulsory education in Vienna. Grandfather had said, "If you want to be a Mrs. Doctor, you will be." And so she was, but it certainly was a pity that she was not permitted to study, and her extraordinary intelligence went to waste.

Oskar and Lili at. the front in the Carpathian Mountains during World War I

My parents' marriage was arranged in the sense that two people were brought together. My two sets of grandparents were second or third cousins and Father just came calling. There was no question that Oskar and Lili would become engaged, nor a need to apply pressure. I understood that this was very much a case of love at first sight. Father was a good-looking young officer, a doctor on leave. Mother was a pretty girl of eighteen from a very good family with a good dowry, not an unimportant consideration for a young doctor who would need money to establish himself after the War. It may seem strange, but I never heard Mother mention another man or boy in her life, or that she was courted by anyone else. The War must have prevented her from having diversions, such as going to dancing school, before she met Father. In retrospect, this absence of a real youth must have influenced Mother's behavior and attitudes in later life.

The way Mother told the story was that Father went back to the Front and they corresponded. For reasons she never really explained, she was in the process of writing him a "Dear John" letter, when Father walked in on a surprise leave[4] and somehow her mind was changed. They were married on September 13, 1917, even though the Singer family was in mourning for her brother, Jacques. Father had to go back on duty, and in wartime one could not wait to see what would happen. There was no honeymoon. Mother went with Father to the base hospital in the Carpathian Mountains in Romania. He no longer had front-line duty. Mother told of the many lonely days and nights she spent waiting for Father to return from the hospital. She was unable to communicate with the Romanian peasants in whose house they were quartered. What a difficult time this must have been for a girl from the comforts of Vienna, just shy of her nineteenth birthday! But Lili was always known to be tough.

---

[4] Editor's note: My grandmother, Lili, told me that my grandfather, Oskar, was granted leave because he had received two telegrams, one saying that his own brother had been killed, which was an error, and a second that Lili's brother, Jacques, had been killed. Reportedly, my grandfather was not in the good graces of his commandant, but the commandant, believing Oskar had suffered a double misfortune, allowed him to return to Vienna on leave. Oskar told Lili he did not expect this commanding officer would be so kind to grant him leave again in order to marry and thus they were married on this visit. They spent their wedding night in a hotel in Vienna and then travelled on a crowded train back to the Front.

Mother eventually returned to Vienna because she was pregnant with my sister.

Felicitas, always called Licci, was born on December 13, 1918, one month after the War was over. Father must have been there because Mother liked to tell how he had promised her a nice birthday present. She had turned twenty just one week earlier on December 7th. He handed Licci to her, saying here is your present. Obviously, she was upset, and had not forgotten this incident all those years later. Sensitivity in this respect was not one of Father's strong suits.

On the Romanian Front in the Carpathian Mountains During World War I

The end of the War and the collapse of the Habsburg Empire brought chaos. Everyone wanted to get home. Father told how a four-hour train ride from Budapest took twenty-four hours. He was so wedged into the train that he could actually not get to the bathroom during the entire trip. With Father's return to civilian life, the search for a place to live and an office began. As always after a war, there was a tremendous housing shortage. Oskar and Lili finally found a place at Taborstrasse 21A, my home for the first eighteen years of my life in Vienna. The location was excellent for a doctor, a main thoroughfare with the trolley car stop literally in front of the house. The apartment was on the third floor, and there was an elevator. It was totally inadequate for a family and an office, but it was all that was available, and it was customary for doctors to have their home and office together.

PAUL HOFFMANN

Taborstrasse 21A circa 1970

There was room for an office, a waiting room, one bedroom, the kitchen and a maid's room. I still wonder how we managed, but this apartment had to suffice until I was about ten years old. If I remember correctly, beds were set up in the office and waiting room at night.

There was a shortage of doctors after the First World War, particularly specialists in venereal disease. On the first Sunday after my parents had moved in, and the shingle hung out, about twenty patients showed up. Obviously things started out well. They apparently stayed that way, until the Great Depression hit Vienna, just like the rest of the world.

4

PAUL: THE EARLY YEARS 1920–1932

MOTHER OFTEN told me that when she became pregnant again in 1920, she really didn't want another child just yet. She was only twenty-one and just didn't think she was ready to cope with having another child. The very cramped quarters we lived in must have factored into her feelings. She had at least two abortions after Licci was born, and Father just wouldn't agree to another one. Good for me. I wonder what motivated Mother to tell me at a young age that I really was not wanted. I think she just didn't think about the impression such a story can make on a child, but her actions and attitudes towards me never bore out what she said. I was certainly her favorite, a problem for my sister Licci until her last days. The jealousy, which certainly impacted on our relationship for the rest of our lives, supposedly started when Licci was sent to stay with Aunt Stella while Mother was in the hospital giving birth to me.

My first actual recollection, and I am not sure how much of what I remember really happened, goes back to the summer of 1922. We were going on vacation to Lake Schliersee near Munich, when I got lost at the train station. I remember standing at the top of the stairs crying. Supposedly, I had broken away from the rest of the family to see the train one more time. I was quickly retrieved by the maid. During a trip to Munich in 1978

I went back to the train station and to Schliersee, but could not rekindle any additional memories.

There is a gap between this memory and the time I clearly remember events in my life, about the time I started school at the age of six in the fall of 1926. However, I can fill in the gaps based on what I have been told. The early 1920s apparently were rather good years for the family. As in the rest of the world, there was business expansion

Paul and Licci circa 1922

and doctors benefited from this increase in commerce as well. Father's practice was active and profitable. The biggest problem right after the War was inflation, which while very bad, was not as catastrophic as it was in Germany, where the money literally lost all of its value. This wiped out the middle class and was probably the main factor in the rise of Hitler, just like the terrible inflation in China after the War greatly helped the Communists come to power.

As I mentioned before, we lived in terribly cramped quarters. The maid was best-off since she had her own room. I really don't remember how we managed, but we lived in one room, my parents' bedroom, during the day while my father worked. There was no other space available and it was not possible to move the practice. The best solution was to get the apartment next door and break through the wall between the two apartments. Eventually, my parents succeeded in doing this, but at great cost. I am sure we children learned one thing; to be very quiet during the day, so that the patients would not hear that there was a family next door. I remember being slapped for being too noisy.

I started school in September 1926 and attended classes in the same building for the next twelve years. I have some recollections of my early school days. I do remember the teacher who I had for the entire four years of grammar school. He seemed very tall and big to a boy of six who was small for his age. He taught everything, except for gym and religion. I was a good pupil, except for gym. I was never athletic. The only sports I did reasonably well were ice skating and swimming, both of which I was taught at an early age.

Since we did not have outside amusements such as radio and television, reading was very important and I read a lot from the time I was very young. The most important entertainment was the weekly soccer game, to which I went with Father, who was a rabid fan. He started to take me when I was six and we went to the last game in Vienna on March 6, 1938, the Sunday before Hitler and his cohorts took over Austria. It is no exaggeration to say that we went to forty to forty five games each year.

When I was six, I started to suffer from a lung related problem, an enlargement of the hilum glands, which, if not taken care of, can lead to something more serious. I had a fever nearly every afternoon. As with people having tuberculosis, it was advisable that I breathe mountain air. I spent, as far as I can remember, one winter and one summer on the Semmering, a mountain resort, two hours by train from Vienna, at an elevation of about 6,000 feet. I definitely remember being there the summer of 1927, because of the unrest in Vienna in July of that year. Mother was very worried because she knew father would find it difficult to stay away from the demonstrations.

What started the strife was a verdict of innocence by a jury in a shooting in which members of the militarized arm of the

Christian Democrats had killed a member of the militarized arm of the Social Democrats. This may seem strange to Americans, but in those days political parties had their own private armies, obviously a very dangerous practice. In Germany, the StormTroopers of the Nazi Party gained control of the streets and terrorized the population, helping Hitler come to power.

In Vienna, the Social Democrats called on their supporters. The crowd converged on the Ministry of Justice. The police lost their heads and fired into the crowd. The crowd then stormed the building and set it on fire. The Social Democrats called a general strike, virtually shutting down the city, leaving it without utilities, and the country, leaving it without railroads. I do not remember how the crisis was eventually resolved, but I remember spending a lot of time counting how many freight cars were on the trains which were visible from the place where we stayed. This incident, less than nine years after the founding of the Austrian Republic, signaled the beginning of the end. The two parties were at loggerheads, and at firearms' length, although I believe that nothing could have saved Austria from Hitler, given the way the world developed in the following ten years.

My recollections of life during the next few years are hazy but become more definite at the time when I entered the gymnasium at the age of ten. The Austrian school system required everyone to go to school until the age of fourteen. At that age, if a child did not continue with school, they normally entered an apprenticeship and had to attend a trade school while working. The decision was normally made at the end of grammar school, age ten, although it was possible to enter the gymnasium at fourteen. This was much more difficult because the curriculum was not as demanding in what was called Volksschule, People's School, for students aged ten to fourteen who would be going into apprenticeships. However, not going to the gymnasium was not that great a disadvantage as it may seem because apprenticeships were the normal career course for such professions as banking and business. In short, there was not the same emphasis on college as we have today in the United States.

In my case, since I was to be a doctor, gymnasium was necessary, and I remember taking the entrance examination in June of 1930 at the age of ten. Since graduating from the gymnasium automatically entitled you to go to the University, the selection process took place during the eight years that were required. How difficult school was can be gathered from the fact that we were forty boys in the first grade, (no coeducational schools in my time), and only eight made it through to the final exams. Since I lived in a static society, this number is not skewed by people moving as is so common in the United States. Our grading system was simple: very good, good, satisfactory and unsatisfactory. An unsatisfactory grade in even one subject, including gym, required repetition of the entire year, although one could take a make-up exam before the beginning of the next school year. While all other schools were free, the gymnasium was not. However, the fees were assessed on the ability to pay based on the family's income tax return. The children of poorer people were often shut out because parents needed the money the children could earn as an apprentice to support their family.

We had school from 8 AM to 1 PM six days a week, and there were no elective subjects during those hours. The curriculum was the same throughout the country. It staggers the mind that the school in Redding, Connecticut, the small rural town where we currently reside, at one time offered as many as two hundred different subjects. The only choices we had were some classes in the afternoon, such as typing and shop classes. Particularly in the upper grades, the homework load was very heavy. You could not get by without doing at least fifteen hours of homework each week. This was very much in keeping with the forty-eight hour work week for everybody else.

Since we lived in a predominantly Jewish district in Vienna, there were usually only four or five non-Jewish boys in the class. In a way, this set somewhat higher standards than in other schools. There generally was no competition among the pupils since there was no ranking. A student who passed with satisfactory grades in all subjects was no worse off than the one who received nothing but very good grades, an impossible feat to accomplish. It was considered bad form to work harder to get a better grade. Rather, your peers expected you to work only as hard as was necessary to pass, and most of the time that was hard enough. Of course, parents cared about your grades and you could not just coast. My grandparents rewarded good report cards with money. Another factor that influenced our performance was the teachers who soon knew whether a pupil was coasting or working hard and demanded more from brighter students. This situation became a problem for me and nearly became my undoing in my junior year, but more on that later on.

Life consisted of school and homework, a walk to my mother's parents' store or home nearly every day and visits to my father's parents. In winter, I went ice skating nearly every day. Since there was no money for vacations during the 1930s, summers were spent at a beach on a dead arm of the Danube. I spent a lot of time with my cousins, Herta and Liesl, Aunt Stella's daughters. I swam, played football and generally whiled away the time.

My first opera experience came in 1930 or 1931, when I was ten or eleven years old, towards the end of the summer before school restarted. I was at the beach and was called home quickly because one of my parents' friends, who was the first violin in the Vienna Opera Orchestra, had gotten tickets. I think I went with Mother. I distinctly remember that the opera was Aida and we hurried to arrive on time because one of the main arias is sung at the beginning of the opera. Thus began my love affair with opera. (I do not remember that movies played any part in my life in those years, and even in later years I do not recall going to the movies very often.)

I have to come back to the Sunday soccer game, not only because it was the highlight of the week, but because it was a great part of my relationship with my father. As Mother used to say, Father and I talked about the previous week's game until Wednesday and the next week's game until Sunday. Rain or snow, we went. He was at least as fervent a fan as I. Many Sundays we would come home hoarse. Sometimes I would worry he would suffer a heart attack from yelling so loud. I refused to join the boy scouts because their Sunday hikes would have conflicted with the games.

I was not a joiner then, and still am not. Organizations and clubs were never my cup of tea. I had a few friends in school, but never won any popularity contests, although I had a few very good friends during my last two or three years in Vienna. My relationship with my parents was very close, maybe because they were home so much of the time. My father played with me a lot. He taught me checkers and chess and I soon beat him regularly. We played nearly every day after I came home from school while we were waiting for lunch, which was served about two in the afternoon. That is, of course, if he did not have any patients, and since these were the Depression years, he unfortunately had a good deal of time. My routine on coming home from school was to first look into the kitchen, say hello to Mother and find out what we would eat for lunch, maybe even grab a little something. If Father was not busy, I would go to his office and tell him about school and then we would go and play for a while. A mechanical soccer game became a real passion. In retrospect, it seems a little ridiculous for the doctor to play this game, but it was fun. I guess on days with few or no patients, my coming home was a very welcome diversion.

In 1930, my parents succeeded in getting the apartment next door and we finally had enough room, although I still did not get my own bedroom. Licci, as the older sibling, got her own room. I slept in the room that served as the ladies waiting room during the day. Because my father's specialty was venereal diseases, it was considered very desirable to have a separate waiting room for ladies. Thus my father's practice took up two big rooms as waiting rooms, his office, his treatment room and a medical appliances room, quite an impressive set up. My parents had their bedroom, Licci had her own room and there was a dining room, which served during the day as the family room. Only after office hours was the place big enough, but standards of space were not quite the same as they are today. Unfortunately, this expansion, which was quite expensive, coincided with the

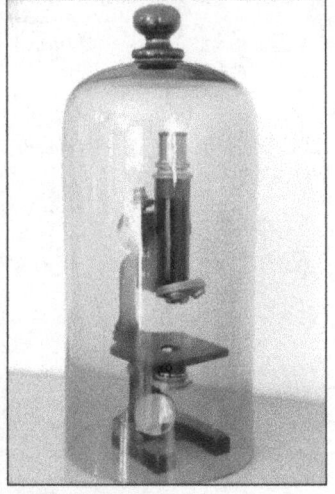

Dr. Oskar Hoffmann in his office and his microscope.

onset of the world-wide Great Depression. During this time, my father's practice suffered a great deal and it was very difficult for us financially until 1937.

5

Storm Clouds Gather: 1933–34

My bar mitzvah took place on December 16, 1933. It was by no means the lavish affair that b'nai mitzvot have become. I doubt that even the richest people in Vienna would have thought it appropriate to put on the type of event middle class people in the United States do today. It would have been considered in bad taste. I was called to the Torah, but because we were not observant, only during the youth service in the afternoon. All I had to do was learn the blessing over the Torah. After the service, we had a party at home. There is not even a set of pictures of the event, unthinkable in the world of the video recording. Most of our relatives came and many of my parents' friends joined us. A number of the guests were from Father's Masonic Lodge, two of whom are still alive at the time of this writing. Presents were modest; no money, mostly books and a chess set. The only really valuable present was a gold watch and chain from my Singer grandparents, which, like the chess set, are still in my possession. It is quite amazing that I was able to preserve both items throughout all my travels. My Singer grandparents were not able to attend the service or reception. Grandfather died about six months after my bar mitzvah. He had been housebound, partially paralyzed for many years. Grandmother had a heart condition and did not go out at all during her last years of her life.

> **HERR UND FRAU DR. OSKAR HOFFMANN**
> BEEHREN SICH MITZUTEILEN, DASS DIE
>
> בר מצוה
>
> IHRES SOHNES
>
> # PAUL
>
> AM SAMSTAG, DEN 16. DEZEMBER 1933, UM 3 UHR, IM TEMPEL
> SEITENSTETTENGASSE, STATTFINDET.
>
> WIEN, II., TABORSTRASSE 21A

Bar Mitzvah Invitation and Certificate

My bar mitzvah seemed to trigger a certain amount of religiousness, as I assume it is supposed to do, but it didn't last long. My attitude towards religion has really not changed much in all these years, despite feeling strongly about my Jewish identity. I am observant to maintain family traditions and to respect my wife Shirley's wishes. As I look back on myself at thirteen, I can see that my basic character and attitudes were well-established by then and have only been tempered by experience and time.

These were not very good years. Times were tough and, unfortunately, Mother would never let us forget it. She suffered greatly from the financial difficulties we, like most people, experienced. Mother complained constantly and I was her confidant. She felt I had to know about every patient and how much they paid or did not pay. Or that father had spent money at the Lodge, or lost some at the card table, and she did not have enough to go to the market. There was not enough money for this and not enough for that. Father's practice was very slow, and he was not a go-getter who would go out and try and improve the situation, which was difficult for a doctor under any circumstances. Father's view was that patients came to a doctor based on his reputation, and that there is nothing a doctor could, or should, do to attract patients. In a way, he was right, but the fact that his younger brother, Richard, was doing very well, in spite of the poor economic conditions, didn't help. Mother's perception was that Father could do more, such as being active in a clinic, for example. Today doctors even advertise, something unheard of in those days and possibly even forbidden by the medical association.

There is no question that things were tight. After all, I knew that the doorbell didn't ring and that Father would owe me my pocket money. Still, we never lacked any necessities, always had a maid, and my parents did not miss their Saturday visits to the coffee house. Looking back, things were not as terrible as mother painted them, but I was deeply influenced by her outlook and at times felt very unhappy. I am sure she bred a considerable amount of insecurity that stayed with me, and led to many unnecessary worries, but it also convinced me that I never wanted to be in that same situation.

As I mentioned before, Father was rather prominent in the Freemasons. This carried a lot of weight in Vienna. The Masons were a secret society, persecuted throughout history. For instance, a Catholic risked excommunication if he joined the fraternity. There is no question that the FreeMasons played a part in the American and French Revolutions with their ideas of equality and freedom. George Washington was a Mason and so was Mozart, as evidenced by his Masonic opera, the Magic Flute. Since the brothers were pledged to secrecy, it was easier to discuss plots in the confines of the Lodge. In Vienna in the 1920s and 1930s, the Masons were generally left-leaning liberal intellectuals and a large percentage was Jewish. I don't recall any non-Jews in my father's Lodge, which had among its members a Member of Parliament, the first violin of the Vienna Opera Orchestra, and a number of medical doctors. Father had become a Mason in 1923 and the Lodge was a very important part of his life. The Lodge met once a week on Wednesdays and I cannot remember an instance when father did not go to a meeting. Nothing could stop him or was more important. In Vienna, I was told the rituals were downplayed and the evenings were primarily taken up with philosophical lectures. I often saw Father working on one of these lectures. After the meeting came dinner and then the brothers were off to the coffee house for cards. Maybe some brothers used the time after the meeting for some other secret rituals. Most of my parents' social life, apart from the family, revolved around the Lodge. Father was Master of the Lodge for many years, a significant honor, but fortunately he refused the position in 1937, because when the Nazis came to power they arrested the masters of every Viennese Masonic Lodge. As I wrote earlier Masonry was anathema to all dictators.

I eventually joined a Lodge in Shanghai and continued to belong to the Humanitas Lodge in New York City. Unfortunately, American Lodges very much concentrate on the rituals, which like all religions are repetitive and become boring after a while, if not outright silly. I am sure it is part of my make-up, plus a considerable change in our way of life thirty years later, that has led to my less enthusiastic embrace of Freemasonry.

The year 1934 was one to remember. There were two

uprisings. In 1933, Fascism became ever-more dominant with the rise to power of Hitler in Germany. Wedged between Fascist Italy and Nazi Germany, Austria also caught this virus and became a dictatorship. The parliament was dissolved by Engelbert Dollfus, who had become Chancellor. He believed his party, the Christian Democrats, was strong enough to transform the Austrian democracy, which had functioned reasonably well since 1919, into the type of state Mussolini had created in Italy. He counted on Mussolini's support and got it. The dictatorship that evolved was by no means as brutal as Hitler's, and maybe even less so than Fascist Italy. Opponents were arrested, the press was controlled, but only to a point, and in general if you minded your own business, and did not care too much about politics, you could continue to live your own life. Dollfus and his successor, Kurt Schuschnigg, tried to instill the Austrians with a certain nationalism as a counterweight to Hitler's Pan Germanism, which found a considerable echo among many Austrians. To them, Hitler was not the monster he really was, but the man who had saved Germany from the Communists. The violent antisemitism of the Nazis was approved and applauded by most Austrians. Dollfus had two serious enemies, the Social Democrats and the Nazis. Both parties were outlawed and, in retrospect, it is clear that Dollfus could not withstand both. That his regime lasted as long as it did, four and a half years, now seems quite surprising.

My memories of the two 1934 uprisings are very vivid. On February 15, 1934, we were let out of school early because the unions, still controlled by the Social Democrats, had declared a general strike. As I walked home, the trolley cars stood still since the workers at the power plants had gone on strike, as did the conductors, drivers and the workers at the gas company. What had led to the strike? The police had raided a club of the Social

Democrats in the provinces to look for and confiscate the arms of the Socialist's private army. No one gives up arms willingly. Shooting started and the situation got out of hand. The forces of Dollfus had long wanted to impose their will and disarm the Socialists. The Social Democrats in turn hoped that they could either wrest control from their opponents, or, at the least, fight them to a standstill and force concessions.

Both parties miscalculated badly. History seems to consist of miscalculations by those in power. The examples are endless. The Right should have known that a defeat of the Left would drive many into the arms of the Ultra-right Nazis. The Left should have known that the two dictators on Austria's borders would not permit a leftist democratic regime to exist for any length of time. They should have known this even if they thought they could defeat the government forces, which included the army and the police.

The tactics of the Social Democrats were also wrong. Over the years the Social Democrats had built workers' housing, particularly in Vienna. This consisted of very large complexes of small apartments, playgrounds, schools and libraries. Each complex housed a few thousand people. These complexes were praised all over Europe for what they tried to accomplish in improving workers' living conditions. However, these buildings also had the aspects of fortresses, and that is what they were meant to be, if so needed. The Socialists, instead of going out into the streets to fight, retreated into their fortresses where weapons were stored. The police and army attempted to flush them out. As they came closer, they were raked with machine gun fire. The army then rolled up artillery and started bombarding the buildings, even though women and children were inside. The Social Democrats probably never believed that the government would shell women and children. They also believed that if ordered to attack, the police, and at least some of the army, would refuse to fire on its own people. They were wrong. It is clear one can never win a fight holed up without hope of relief from the outside. The fighting continued for three days, mostly concentrated around the buildings, but some of it in the streets. When it was all over, the government had won. Some of the leaders of the uprising were hanged, others jailed, and the Fascists were now in complete control of Austria.

In our house, all sympathies were with the Social Democrats. Father was always a Socialist and Mother had her hands full persuading him from going out and helping the Social Democrats, if for no other reason but to serve as a doctor. Obviously, he could have been shot and certainly would have been arrested for helping the opposition. For me, just past thirteen years of age, this was very exciting. One could hear the cannons and gunfire close by in the streets.

Electricity and gas were restored fairly quickly. Even though this was the middle of the winter, I have no recollection of being cold. We had some coal stored and I think a patient of Father's helped out with emergency supplies. School was closed for about a week, and I am sure we did not go out of the house for several days. Strange as it may seem, at least on the surface, for those not shelled, injured, or arrested, life returned to normal fairly quickly.

After Dollfus had crushed the Social Democrats, he turned his attention to the Nazis. At that point, he had Mussolini's protection against Hitler. I remember Wednesday July 25, 1934. I was planning to go to a very important soccer game between our favorite team and an Italian team. Father would not be going with me. He had office hours and no exceptions could be made. It was about midday when we heard that fighting had broken out in the provinces between the Nazis and the Austrian Army.

Father, with some difficulty, persuaded me not to go to the game, which, as I remember, went on anyway. It certainly was not safe to be out on the streets. There was no fighting in the streets of Vienna. The Nazis had confined their action to the Chancellery, where they shot Dollfus and literally let him bleed to death.

This uprising was put down somewhat more quickly than the February uprising. There continued to be little fighting in Vienna, where the Nazis were not yet very strong. This time, our sympathies had to be with the government, whether or not we liked it.

The July uprising signaled the beginning of the end, if one believed that Hitler would continue in power. The hope and false speculation at that point was that the Germans, particularly the German Officer Corps, would not stand much longer for this low-class ruffian, Adolph Hitler. This was obviously also the thinking of Mussolini, who had amassed his troops at Austria's southern border to ward Hitler off. (I really am not trying to write a history of Austria, I did this in my thesis which I was required to write to graduate from Aurora University in Shanghai. Unfortunately, it is in French. Maybe I'll translate it one day.) However, it is impossible to write about one's life in the 1930s and 1940s without discussing politics, because it was the political events which shaped my life.

6

LIFE WITHIN TURMOIL: 1935—1937

THE MOMENTOUS and far reaching events of 1934, quickly receded in the swirl of ordinary life. I was fourteen, in ninth grade, and school was probably the most important part of life, simply because so much time was spent at school and studying. I was a good pupil, but not outstanding. In retrospect, it is clear that the system did generally not permit excellent grades. The demands were so high that hardly anyone achieved an outstanding record.

The opera and the theater became ever more important parts of my life. Some of the opera tickets came from my father's friend, some from school, but I also bought my own standing room tickets. I vividly remember seeing Franz Lehar conduct his latest operetta, Giuditta, with Richard Tauber. I remember seeing the great Walter Slezak, who already was a star of stage and screen in America. There was a performance of Rheingold, during which I irritated the people around me by trying to eat peanuts. One of my school friends was a Wagnerian, and with the arrogance of youth

Fourteen Year Old Paul

denigrated all other composers, including my favorite Italians, such as Puccini and Verdi. We had bitter arguments.

My theater experiences were primarily with the classical repertory. There were student performances at the State Theater on Saturday afternoons. Sometimes I went with my sister, Licci, sometimes with friends. Most of the performances were of the German classics, such as Friedrich Schiller and Gotthold Lessing, but I also saw some Shakespeare in its German translation; good, but nothing like the English originals.

At about that time, my parents taught me bridge and I started to play with my friends. I always loved the game and became a Life Master when I retired. I was a voracious reader. I loved Greek mythology and read all of Homer. I would read about everything, and while I do not remember everything, I do not think that matters. What counts is that I absorbed many ideas which probably helped me in thinking and forming my own views in later life.

Both of my grandfathers died in 1935 at the age of eighty one. I cannot write about their deaths, without commenting on what I perceive to be one of the serious problems in our society. We now go to incredible lengths to keep even a brain-dead octogenarian alive at great financial cost to the country and emotional cost to the family. My grandfathers were allowed to die in relative peace. Grandfather Singer, who had spent several years in a wheelchair, suffered another stroke and lapsed into a coma. No measures were taken. I don't know that anything could have been done as the machines used today didn't exist. He died within the week.

Grandfather Hoffmann developed prostate cancer. The only treatment consisted of pain medication since it was too late for an operation, and I assume one did not operate on an eighty-one-year-old man in those days. When his condition worsened and the pain became excessive, the four doctors in the family, my father, Uncle Richard, and the two grandsons who had already completed their medical studies, Franz and Erich, decided to end Grandfather's life with an extra strong morphine injection. I think it was the humane thing to do and it is my wish that one of these days our society will allow euthanasia. I do not think that euthanasia was permitted then, but nobody knew. The two funerals were the first I had ever attended and brought me face to face with death in the family for the first time. I felt the loss of Grandfather Hoffmann more, as I had a closer relationship with him.

After the debacle of the Socialists in 1934, Father started to support the Communist underground. In addition to giving money, he, together with a good friend, a dentist, acted as a drop-off for Communist couriers. It is interesting to reflect that it did not seem inconsistent to my father and his friend to be Communists and Freemasons at the same time, knowing that the Communists, like all other dictatorships, suppressed Freemasonry. I suppose he had to have a cause. In 1936, the Communist Party was outlawed by the Austrian dictatorship. Our dentist was arrested for helping the Communist Party. Panic struck the Hoffmann household. Fortunately, no one talked and Father was spared. Mother put an end to father's affiliation with the Communists by threatening to leave him if he continued his party activities. It was fortunate that he chose to step away because had he continued up to Hitler's takeover, he would certainly have been arrested. Father would not have been one to survive a concentration camp. Our dentist was eventually released and escaped to the United States after Hitler invaded Austria.

My sister Licci also got involved with a Communist underground cell. Licci took me along to a meeting of the "cell". This was really dangerous, because if the police had discovered the meeting we would all have landed in jail. I can't remember what was discussed, but I do remember that I came away with the knowledge that this was not for me and that these were not the kind of people I wanted to associate with. I never went back. My relationship with Licci was not improved by my political attitude.

We eventually found out that Licci's interest in the cell was at least partially due to a fellow who had turned her head. She was only seventeen years old and he was quite a bit older. I remember the Sunday afternoon when she came to my grandparent's apartment from a supposed hike in the woods. Mother discovered red marks on her neck, clearly caused by a man's mustache. (Mother would know since Father had a mustache.) The reaction to her scandalous behavior seems unreal in today's permissive world. She was totally grounded to the point that, I, or someone else went to pick her up from school every day for a month or so.

As I write this and have seen the collapse of Communism. I am proud that I rejected this ideology when I was in my teens, even though my father and sister supported it. Father was an idealist who fervently believed in the ideas of Karl Marx and Friedrich Engels. Granted, on paper their ideas sound very good, but when put into practice they do not work and lead to a dictatorship that is no different than a fascist dictatorship. There was always the argument that the end justifies the means because the end will be a just world without poor people. We now know that seventy years of Communism in the Soviet Union did not succeed and two generations would seem long enough to prove if the system could be successful. I am sure there are still many, including some in this country, who will argue that Communism can succeed, that it was just bad people who perverted the principles of the ideology. There are always those who will not accept reality.

As I wrote earlier, Licci was always jealous of my relationship with Mother. Now, in these tumultuous years, she often derided and chided me for being too ambitious and materialistic, as if ambition is a character fault and materialism is wrong. If not practiced to excess, which I certainly never did, I still consider these characteristics as helpful and useful in life. I don't want to leave the impression that we didn't get along at all, or did not care for each other, but for a person as thin-skinned as I am, it was not easy to be put down all the time.

One standard accusation was that I was too selfish. I don't think this is really true. I think I always drew a narrow circle around my family as my most important interest. Unfortunately, at least for the first forty years of my life, there was very little room for anything else. I have never been the classical liberal do-gooder, but have always believed, and still believe, in one's responsibility to take care of oneself and one's family. (I will return to Licci many times, but I believe her jealousy, and my hurt over her lack of understanding of what I believe to be my true character carried forward to our adult life. That some of this was never discussed and really brought out into the open is really a pity, but I think this is the way people are.)

The years 1935 through 1937 were the last years of my youth. Girls began to play an important part in my life. I actually had my first little girlfriend when I was nine years old at the skating rink. I lost track of her over the years, and she became a very short romantic interlude when we met again in 1938, shortly before I had to leave Vienna. I started having more steady girlfriends in 1936 when I was sixteen. We would neck but that was about it. Sex among teenagers was not anywhere near as common as it has become today. Yes, sex was a preoccupation in the minds of boys of that age, but there was more talk than action.

During the first semester of my junior year, I ran into a difficult problem. Even fifty-five years later, I ascribe it to a combination

Paul's Half Year Report Card for 1936/37

of bad luck and two crazy teachers. One of them, for reasons I still don't understand, took a real dislike to me. It was his view that I didn't work up to my potential and should be punished for it. He was so prejudiced against me, that after I had graduated and left Vienna, he met father in a bookstore. When told that I had left for Shanghai he commented, "He will never amount to anything." He was obviously wrong, but it characterizes the man, a Jew himself, to say this to a father who had just sent both his children to foreign countries. He must have been crazy.

He was the French teacher, and in my junior year also took over our Latin course, never one of my better subjects. He failed me in both subjects at the end of the first semester. Latin may have been partly deserved, but French was pure spite. The third failing grade came in descriptive geometry. Admittedly, I never understood the subject very well, but I had passed the test. The last class before the end of the semester, the professor called some of us to the board to solve a difficult problem. Those of us who could not solve the problem were told we would fail based on this one oral question. This seems absolutely irrational by today's standards, but that's how these little Caesars behaved. I am sorry to have to say that this professor was also Jewish.

The hue and cry in the Hoffmann house when I came home with my February report card was spectacular. Frankly, the report card foretold disaster since it seemed unlikely that I would pass all three subjects at the end of the year and therefore would have to repeat the whole year. The thought was shocking to all concerned and would have been a lifelong setback since I would not have graduated from high school before leaving Vienna. I was accused of being lazy, too interested in girls and various other sins. Each of which may have had some truth to it. I remember one girl very vividly from that period. Her name was Erika, she was a year younger than I and she was adorable. We mostly went for walks in the park. There was some petting on the benches, but nothing more serious. I was crazy about her. I am not sure whether my school problems broke this up,

Erica Lowy – September 1936   Paul and Erica at the park

but I think that must have been what happened. (Thankfully, she survived the War and found her way to Israel.) Father was generally more supportive of me than Mother; maybe he had a better understanding of what goes on with sixteen-year-old boys. After all, he had a similar experience in his senior year. The secret plan, not really told to me until it was all over, was that if I failed, not to let me repeat the year but to have me attend a private school that would somehow arrange things so that I would graduate as scheduled.

I was able to pull off the unbelievable, passed all three subjects during the second semester and was promoted into my senior year. The summer of 1937 was my reward for all my troubles during the year. It was probably the best summer of my life and the last one I did not have to work until the summer of 1989, when I fully retired. An organization in Vienna arranged for young people to spend their summers in Hungary with host families who had children of the same age. The purpose was for the Hungarian children to learn German since it was important for Hungarians to have German as a second language. Both Licci and I went. My first two attempts in 1935 and 1936, had not ended well. In 1935, I was sent to Tokay to a very religious Jewish family, who, for me, lived under rather primitive conditions, including a lack of indoor plumbing. I now understand what nice people they were, but for a boy of not yet fifteen, the culture shock was too great and I went home after two weeks. The next summer I went to Budapest, to another very nice family with two boys and was enjoying my summer, but got sick with what was probably flu after four weeks. I was misdiagnosed as having something rather more serious and was sent home.

But 1937 worked. I went to Sarospatak. Licci had been there the year before. Sarospatak was a small town of perhaps ten thousand people, in the northeastern part of Hungary near the Czech and Polish borders. Transportation was mostly on foot and for longer distances, people used horse and carriages. Some boys had bicycles, and there must have been the odd car. During the school year the town was full of boys since there were some private schools. It was the center for the Tokay region, famous for its wines and grapes.

I was placed with the Szabo family. The family consisted of Dr. Szabo, a general practitioner, his wife, a lovely lady, and two boys, one two years younger than I and the other seven or eight years old. I remember this summer so well. I arrived in the afternoon, after having spent the night in Budapest, but I hadn't slept very much. I had gone to an amusement park with one of the girls from the group. The other fellows with whom I shared the room weren't very kind to me when I came in about two in the morning. There was a lot of ribbing and other nonsense. My train left fairly early the next day. I remember being picked up after a six or seven-hour train ride, for a distance of no more than one hundred miles, by Mrs.Szabo in her horse and carriage,

Sandor, Gabor, Frau Szabo and Paul – Sarospatak – Summer 1937

which she drove herself. When asked what I wanted, I said a glass of milk and to go to sleep. Well, they couldn't wake me up until eleven o'clock the next morning. That is when I was first introduced to the rest of the family.

What I remember most about the first day is that we went to the beach on the riverfront. As I swam out into the water that first day, a blond girl named Aggie swam towards me. This initial meeting set the course for the rest of the summer. Aggie was the daughter of the local pharmacist and a year or so older than me. Her fiancé was in the army and she had apparently decided to lay claim to me while he was gone. Later in the summer her fiancé, who must have been home on leave, confronted me at a dance and challenged me. He was at least five years older and dressed in the uniform of a lieutenant. Fortunately, I was able to laugh off his comments without ill effect. It was a marvelous summer; the carriage drives, swimming and dances. And then there was the food and wine, I nearly ate myself sick on the Tokay grapes in the Szabo's vineyards. In short, I had the time of my life. When I left, the plan was to return the next summer, but Hitler intervened. The Szabos and some other families sent parcels to us in Vienna and in general conducted themselves like the marvelous people they were. After we left Vienna, we lost touch. There is little doubt that most, if not all of these people, like nearly all Hungarian Jews, were transported to Hitler's concentration camps and exterminated. Even today, the thought of all these young people being tortured and killed, makes me sick.

October 1937 brought the death of Grandmother Singer. She finally succumbed to her ailing heart. It was an event of considerable importance for our family. The focus for the daily family gatherings was lost. I was so very fond of Grandmother Singer. In 1936, I had lived with her for several weeks because Licci contracted scarlet fever and I could not live at home until she was no longer infectious. Strangely, I never got sick, but two or three fellows who sat next to me in school did. I enjoyed my stay and won a considerable amount of money playing cards with Grandmother.

Grandmother's death also had important financial consequences. Mother inherited a substantial amount of money that had been in trust until Grandmother died. Licci and I, like the other cousins, inherited a share in the large rental property owned by our grandparents. The revenue for each of us was not large, but sufficient to be a very nice supplementary income. At the same time, Father's practice showed signs of improving, just as business conditions around the world improved spurred by preparations for war. But as happened so often during the first thirty years of my life, when things started to look up, the roof fell in.

During 1937, the Nazis increased pressure on Austria with the declared aim of annexation. There were many reasons for this. The most obvious was to increase Hitler's power, but there was the longstanding wish for a greater Germany, encompassing all the Germans in Europe. This was not Hitler's idea, he just adopted it. As a matter of fact, the Austrians, after the dismemberment of the Habsburg Empire in 1919, had freely voted to become part of Germany, but avoided this actuality for two more decades. Finally, Hitler's personal experiences played an important part in the eventual annexation. Hitler wanted to show his homeland what the poor house painter, who never got any recognition in Vienna, could achieve.

As I wrote earlier, the Italians had saved Austria in 1934. At that time, Mussolini still appeared to be the stronger of the two dictators, but by the end of 1937, the balance of power had shifted in Hitler's favor.

I have my own theory about what may have helped Mussolini finally decide to give in to Hitler. In November 1937, an international soccer match between Italy and Austria took place in Vienna. Father and I were there on this cold and rainy Sunday. The Italians were always unpopular in Austria, particularly since the First World War when they renounced their alliance with Austria and joined the French and English. The Austrians believed they were stabbed in the back, and they probably were right. Many Austrians had died on the Italian front, including my Uncle Jacques, my mother's brother.

It did not help that as part of the peace treaty Italians got the Southern part of Tyrol as a reward. As always, all hell broke loose in the stands as soon as the Italian players took the field. The Italian players responded with very rough play. The referee lost control and eventually the game was called off. Later that day, a mob assembled at the Italian embassy to protest and windows were broken. I believe Mussolini's proverbial vanity was hurt and he decided that the Austrians did not deserve his protection. I am sure the annexation of Austria was inevitable, but the events of November 1937 may have hastened the events of March 12, 1938, the Anschluss, the day Hitler marched his troops into Austria.

7

1938: The Worst Year

THE YEAR 1938 was certainly the worst year of my life. Father, as happened so often, showed an excellent grasp of the danger. In January 1938, when Kurt Schuschnigg, the Austrian chancellor, was "ordered" to visit Hitler in his lair in Berchtesgaden, Father predicted that annexation was imminent. He asked Mother not to spend any more money on refurbishing the apartment, which she had started to do with the money she had inherited from her mother, even though the apartment really needed a sprucing up after the long Depression years. Why did father not act on his intuition and decide to leave Austria? This question is best answered by another question. How does an established fifty-year-old doctor, with a son in his senior year of high school and a daughter finishing her secondary education, decide to give up everything, including his and his wife's family? There was not enough ready cash to go to another country for a few weeks to see what would happen. Regardless of the economic impact, the school situation for Licci and me made that a most difficult decision. I doubt that serious immediate consideration was given to such a drastic step. As it turned out, a reasonable plan to liquidate and leave, could not proceed as quickly as the events that ensued.

The political situation deteriorated very rapidly. The Nazis demonstrated constantly and started to take over the streets. The government vacillated between giving in and taking a stand, but on March 9, 1938 the Austrian Republic finally decided to say "NO" to Hitler. Schuschnigg called a referendum for Sunday, March 13th, on the question of unification with Germany. This forced Hitler's hand. He could not risk that the referendum would go against him. The propaganda on both sides was deafening.

March 12th, 1938 was Father's 50th birthday. All had been planned. Coincidentally, that Saturday night was also the night of my senior class performance and I had been chosen to be the master of ceremonies. My parents, my girlfriend Edith, Licci and her boyfriend would attend the performance and afterwards, we would all go to a nightclub to celebrate Father's birthday. I still remember the name of the club, Bodega. Needless to say, none of this happened. By Friday, March 11th, tension had risen to the boiling point. Only a few people still believed that the plebiscite would take place. The streets, particularly in the center of town, were full of demonstrators.

That Friday afternoon, I set out to pick up Edith from her job. She had been my girlfriend for about six months. In retrospect, I think I was much more in love with Edith than she was with me. While we were the same age, she was a working girl in an office, and I was still a school boy. That made a big difference in those days. I still remember the 1937 New Year's party at her house, a rather naughty affair. Her parents swore there would not be another party at their house. Unfortunately, how right they were! There were no more parties,

Edith – Vienna – May 28, 1938

but for a very different reason.

To understand my experiences that afternoon, it helps to understand a little about the geography of Vienna. The inner city, where all the government buildings are, is ringed by a very wide boulevard, the Ringstrasse. Along the Ringstrasse are all the impressive buildings like the Opera House, the State Theater, City Hall, the Emperor's Palace and many others. One side of the boulevard was flanked by an arm of the Danube. We lived on the other side of that arm, about a ten-minute walk from the inner city. Edith's office was on the opposite side of the inner city. My normal path would have been straight through the center of the city. On the city side of the bridge, which I had to cross, I was stopped by the police who had sealed off the center of the city, ostensibly to prevent demonstrations. I remember the policeman advising me, rather kindly, not to go on. But I had a date and pressed on. I walked around the city on the Ringstrasse and met Edith. With the bravado of youth, we decided to see what was going on and managed to get into the center of the city, where the St. Stephen's Cathedral and the Palace of the Archbishop of Vienna are located.

This area had become the focus of the demonstrations. On the Palace side of the square were those people who chose to stay loyal to the government. On the other side were the Nazi supporters. Insults and threats were hurled across the street. Suddenly, around six o'clock, the Nazis stopped shouting as if to say, "You can shout all you want, we won."

I sensed trouble and we started on our way home. I had guessed right. Schuschnigg had abdicated and Hitler had announced that German troops were marching into Austria to protect his followers. From what I heard later, it was lucky that we left when we did. Soon all hell broke loose. The police were prepared. They took swastika armbands out of their pockets and put them on. Anyone who looked remotely Jewish was beaten.

My luck held, as it would hold over the next six-and-a-half months. I managed to get Edith home safely and arrived at my apartment house at about seven o'clock in the evening. The pictures from this evening are indelibly impressed in my mind. The hate distorted faces yelling at each other, the somewhat tipsy bereft man crying, and as I went up the stairs, I met Father coming down, going out to buy cigarettes. He was white as a sheet and all he said was, "It is all over." At that moment, I do not think he fully realized how terrible things would be. Life as we knew it had come to an end and it was brought home to us with full force the next day.

Saturday morning, March 12, 1938, Father decided he had to find out how my cousin, Kurt, was doing in his porcelain store in the city. I would not let him go alone. It was a brisk clear morning. Overnight the streets had become a sea of swastika flags and nearly everyone who was not Jewish wore a swastika in his or her lapel. This clearly disavows the myth fostered on history by some that Austria was occupied by the Germans. Nonsense! An overwhelming portion of the population welcomed Hitler, and in many cases, deliriously so. On our way, many passers-by shouted "Dirty Jews" or worse at us. When we got to Kurt's store, we found that the porter, who had secretly been a member of the Storm Troopers, the infamous SS, had taken over the store.

The situation rapidly became intolerable for Jews. Within a week the maid had to leave. She was not permitted to serve in a Jewish household. Jewish doctors were forbidden to treat non-Jewish patients. When the schools reopened after a week, all Jewish teachers had been fired and the school I attended had become a Jewish school. All non-Jewish students had been transferred out and Jewish boys from other schools were moved to my school. You would have thought all Jews were infected with a contagious disease, such as leprosy or AIDS. But that was not all. The Nazi propaganda ascribed to Jews was even worse than carrying a terrible disease. Jews were arch criminals to be feared and hated, responsible for all the ills of society.

It was a stroke of luck that the Nazis permitted us to finish the school year. It was the last year Jewish children could go to school in Naziland. I was able to graduate from the gymnasium; a major benefit in later years. Obviously, it was not easy to concentrate on school under the circumstances. There are a couple of incidents that stick in my mind. One of our teachers, generally considered a mild-mannered guy, one day decided to give a wildly antisemetic speech. It is hard to understand why he would do this in front of a class of Jewish fellows. After listening for a while I raised my hand and asked to be excused saying, "I can't stand it anymore". I was deliberately ambiguous; it could be inferred that I had to go to the bathroom. On another day, he reproached a group of us boys for smoking in front of the school. I responded that I really didn't care anymore.

Dr. Hoffmann's Prescription Pad stamped with "For Medical Treatment Exclusively for Jews."

An interesting contrast was our mathematics teacher, who reputedly was the brother-in-law of Hitler's second in command, Hermann Goering. Supposedly, it was on the strength of this association that he became the principal. On the other hand, he was very fair and I never heard him make any antisemetic remarks.

I especially disliked the gym teacher who was another rabid Nazi. I heard somewhere that he died in the War on the Russian front. (I hope he suffered significantly before he joined the others in hell.) Anyway, I passed all the exams. Only written exams were given; fortunately they dispensed with the oral exams that year. So, at the end of May 1938 I graduated and was out of school. However, instead of a pleasant vacation before entering University, I, like all Jews, was faced with the question of how and where to emigrate to, before we would be sent to a concentration camp. Life was intolerable. Going out of the house was dangerous since you never knew what would happen to you. You could be spat upon, beaten without provocation or simply carted off to jail, just because you were a Jew. Many Jews were stopped in the street and forced to scrub slogans off the street, with the crowd watching gleefully and shouting insults. This pastime was particularly popular shortly after the Nazi takeover when pavements and walls had been used as canvases for propaganda slogans. Well-dressed women were especially attractive to the mobs. Many of these women walked away with bloody knees and raw hands, since extra amounts of lye were added to the cleaning solution. Bloody faces were also not unusual.

I was caught only once. One Saturday afternoon, early in May, I had just finished carrying firewood up from the cellar when two Storm Troopers rang the doorbell and asked that "the young man" come with them. Obviously somebody had fingered me. How would they otherwise have known that there was a young man in the apartment? They had rung the bell of the office and said "Let's go". Mother tried to stall them, which would not have helped, so I took my coat and walked out the other of our two front doors. As I look back upon this situation, and other dangerous incidents in my life, some, including the one described here, were life threatening. I am still amazed how outwardly calm I was able to act. My reaction after the danger was over, would be a different matter.

The Nazis had decided that this Saturday was to be Jewish Boycott Day and that those Jewish businesses that had not yet been taken over should be pointed out so that, God forbid, a non-Jew would not be tempted to enter the establishment. A small Jewish coffee house was located in our apartment building with its entrance facing the street. I was given a sign on which was written "Jewish Establishment" and some very rude anti-Semitic words. I joined two or three others already there holding similar signs. From time to time, the Nazis grabbed another Jewish person to replace the person who had been standing there the longest.

We were surrounded by a jeering crowd, hurling insults at us. I remember one yelling at me, "Look at the hands of the Jewish pig. They show he never did any work". During the whole time I stood there, I was wondering what would happen if I hit a member of the mob over the head with the sign. I am glad I didn't. At the very least, I would have been beaten severely. After about three quarters of an hour they caught one of our neighbors, a man my father's age to replace me. I offered to stay for him, but they would not let me. I remember the Storm Trooper saying to me, "Go home. You are a brave boy". I did, and threw up. This was the first, but not the last time I had this physical reaction once danger had passed. It is not difficult to imagine what my parents went through, not knowing whether I would come back, and if I did, whether I would be in one piece. As a matter of fact, I was lucky. Shortly thereafter, the mob that I had been facing got out of hand. Not only were people beaten, they were made to clean toilets with their bare hands and even more appalling and humiliating acts.

Uncle Ernst, Mother's brother, was arrested. Licci's boyfriend, neighbors and friends disappeared and nobody knew why. The restrictions on Jews became tighter and tighter. I don't know how my parents managed to keep our household going. Father did have some Jewish patients, but everyone was using up whatever savings they had. Access to bank accounts was also restricted. But, as always, there were people worse off than us. The Jews in the most far eastern province of Austria, the Burgenland, were given forty-eight hours to leave with what they could carry. They naturally came to Vienna, and Licci and I went door to door collecting money and clothing from the other Jews in our building to help these refugees.

At home, all discussions centered around the latest atrocities and disappearances and where and how to emigrate. We had no connections outside Austria and no country opened its borders. Some people were lucky enough to have relatives in the United States. Some countries sold visas, primarily Central American and South American countries, like the Dominican Republic. The world was a much larger and stranger place than today where the jet plane, television and international telephone communications have greatly increased people's mobility and understanding of the world. Except for during World War I, 1914-18, my parents had never been more than two hundred miles from Vienna. What one knew of other countries was from books or pictures. I do not remember ever seeing a black or Asian person in Vienna. I knew of Joe Louis, a black American boxer, beating the German Max Schmeling, and of the success of black athletes, particularly Jesse Owens at the Berlin Olympics.

Father decided that the children should leave first. As it turned out, that was a good decision, but luck played a big part in making it so. Licci's fate was quickly settled. England opened its borders to young women who were willing to serve as maids or nannies and Licci was accepted into this program. On Mother's side, my cousin, Kitty, went with a children's transport, the Kindertransport through Holland to England. On the Hoffmann side, Erich Hohenberg's wife had a connection in England. Erich was able to bring his brother, Kurt, and his new wife Rosl to England, as well. They also took Grandmother Hoffmann and their mother, Bertha, along. Eventually we had quite a contingent in England. Grandmother, who was about eighty, was already senile, probably due to Alzheimer's disease. She committed suicide shortly after they arrived, by jumping from a window. Not much later Aunt Bertha, who had suffered from depression since her husband's death, also took her life in the same manner. Were they also Hitler's victims? Grandmother may not have been, but I think Bertha most likely was.

Uncle Richard managed to get visas to the United States for his family. Uncle Fritz and family went to his wife Maltchi's brothers in Czechoslovakia and eventually, with Richard's help, made it to the United States. My cousin Franz, through a connection on his wife's side of the family, managed to get visas for himself, his wife, and mother, my Aunt Ila, to New Zealand. There was a shortage of doctors in New Zealand and the fact that Franz was a doctor helped to obtain their visas. Uncle Eduard, who suffered from multiple sclerosis, could not escape. When my parents offered to take their teenage daughter with them to Shanghai, his wife refused. The whole family disappeared.

On Mother's side, Uncle Ernst and his family somehow got visas to the United States with the help of a Jewish organization. My cousin Lotte, and her husband illegally crossed the border into France. When the Germans overran France, they were separated. Lotte ended up in a concentration camp in Belgium, where she met her second husband, Bernard. I was able to get my Aunt Margit and her husband to Shanghai. My cousin, Fred, was sent to his father's cousin in Washington, DC. Unfortunately, his parents, my Aunt Steffi and Uncle Arpad, held on to the hope that they would be able to join Fred in America and did not accept our offer to come to Shanghai. I know we could've helped them get there. They died in Auschwitz.

I recount again what happened to individual family members to characterize the atmosphere that prevailed as the world as we knew it was shattered and our family was torn apart. Of course, one's friends also left, if they could. My girlfriend, Edith, went to Czechoslovakia where she had family. In the end, one had to be happy for those who were able to leave no matter how much it hurt. Suddenly, the world that had centered on Vienna, now included London, England, Christchurch, New Zealand, Washington, D.C., and soon Shanghai, China.

Plans for me to leave were explored constantly. In preparation for leaving we took English lessons. I was also required to learn some kind of trade. Operating a knitting machine was thought to be a good idea. I was as good with my hands then as I am now. I was never able to learn properly, and the one attempt I made to use this skill in Shanghai, ended in disaster. I lasted less than two days.

The first plan was to cross the border illegally into Czechoslovakia to join Uncle Fritz. It was called illegal, because no exit or entry visas were obtained, but it seems trying to save one's life can hardly be termed illegal. This attempt failed because a night or two before I was to go, the German border guards caught some people with very terrible results. A Jewish organization had organized another escape route. One would board a boat on the Danube in the middle of the night. By morning, the boat would be in Hungarian waters and then continue to the Black

Sea. There, the passengers would be transferred to a bigger ship to go to Palestine. Again, something happened just before I was to leave and this plan failed too. Aunt Stella and her family were able to make this trip later on and safely arrived in Palestine. How different my life and that of many others would have been had this plan succeeded!

The search for a place to go continued. In the meantime, life was getting worse. There was no escape from the daily misery. Jews could not go to any public place such as a theater or movie. One Sunday, in August of 1938, Licci and I got so fed up with being cooped up in the house, we stupidly decided to go rowing on an arm of the Danube. Within minutes, we were spotted and we heard cries of "Dirty Jews! Drown them!" from other boats. We quickly rowed back and counted ourselves lucky to get back home safely. No wonder any place in the world began to look good to us.

8

LEAVING FOR SHANGHAI

ONE MORNING, late in August 1938, shortly after a visitor informed us about the possibility of going to Shanghai, Father and I, without telling Mother, went to the Italian shipping line, Lloyd Triestino. We managed to purchase a second-class ticket for me on the *Conte Verde*. The ship would be leaving Trieste on October 31, 1938. There were only a few boats to China and tickets went very quickly once it became evident that this was a viable escape route.

Paul – August 1938

In 1938, Shanghai was an open city. It included an International Settlement ruled under a treaty with the Chinese by a Municipal Council. The Council was in the hands of the British and Americans with a strong Japanese contingent. It had its own international police force, United States Marines and British soldiers were stationed there, but it had no immigration policy. A visa was not required for entry; anyone who arrived in Shanghai could stay. All that was needed was a boat ticket and a German exit visa since Austria had been annexed as a province of Germany.

When Father and I came home and told Mother what we had

done, she accused father of having gone crazy. How could her boy go to China alone? China was on the other side of the world, a one month trip away!

I still wonder why I agreed to go. The furthest distance I had been away from home was to Hungary, about one-hundred-and-fifty miles from Vienna. Maybe it was due to the innocence of youth, plus a certain sense of adventure, but I think mostly it was the knowledge that it was impossible to stay. Now the preparations for me and Licci to leave got under way in earnest.

The main task was to get an exit visa. You would have thought that the Nazis would be happy to get rid of the Jews. But it seemed that torturing Jews made them happier. Everyone had to obtain a number of documents before being issued a one-way passport. Among the papers were a tax document that proved you owed no taxes, a document that you had never been in trouble with the law and some other papers I do not remember. Obtaining each of these documents meant standing in line for days, sometimes through the night. One reason for these long waits was the number of people seeking emigration papers, but more so, it was due to the callousness of the Nazis. No additional staff were added to help the process, and the slowdown appeared deliberate, to make us as miserable as possible. It was not unusual to stand in line through the night to be told that on that day only the first twenty people would be dealt with. Or, a person might reach the desk and be told that a document lacked this or that signature. Standing in line was not free of danger. People were attacked, particularly at night. (This experience, plus a similar experience in the Hongkew ghetto with the Japanese in Shanghai explains my total aversion to standing in line for anything.) Eventually we got our passports. Mine was made out to Paul Israel Hoffmann. Licci's was made out to Felicitas Sara Hoffmann. The name Israel for men and Sara for women was inserted into every passport issued to a Jew. The Nazis wanted to make sure that everyone who saw it would know that the bearer was a Jew. The passport became invalid once you left Germany and you became a stateless person.

In the meantime, we had discovered that Shanghai was not quite so forbidding a place. Richard's brother-in-law, Max Ehrlich, had married a Russian Jewish woman. The family name was Ossinovsky. Her brother, Joseph Ossin, lived in Shanghai with his family. He was an engineer for Otis Elevator and the Ehrlichs had already left to join the Ossins in Shanghai. Thus, I left with the Ossin's address in hand. I have so much more to relate about these marvelous people, but will save this for my arrival in Shanghai.

A second connection developed through a friend of Aunt Ila, Bertha Ellig. Her brother had gone to Shanghai on business in the 1920s, married an English woman and remained there. Miss Ellig's brother died about the time Hitler marched into Vienna and Miss Ellig was going to Shanghai, both to claim her inheritance and to escape Austria. As luck would have it, she was booked on the same boat as me. This very much relieved my mother's worries. Here was someone to take care of her little boy. It turned out that it would be the other way around and in a number of instances, I would be taking care of Miss Ellig.

War nearly broke out in September of 1938. Hitler, having swallowed Austria without any noticeable protest by the world, correctly guessed that he could proceed with his program for a Greater Germany as laid out in his book, "Mein Kampf". His next target was "rescuing" the Germans living in Czechoslovakia. The usual propaganda barrage of atrocities committed by the Czechs against the "poor" Germans started and reached ridiculous proportions. To protect the Germans, Hitler amassed his troops on the border between Germany and Czechoslovakia. The

Western powers, mainly France and England, had guaranteed the Czech border and were obliged to go to war if Hitler marched into Czechoslovakia. Intense negotiations started and it soon became clear that the Democracies were not willing, or able, to risk another world war. How wrong they were! It would have been easier to defeat Hitler had the Allies held firm a year earlier. He may not even have gone to war. Well, history has recorded how Hitler duped the English and French. No one who lived through those days will ever forget the words of the British Prime Minister, Neville Chamberlain, upon returning from his meeting with Hitler. "Peace in our time" is what he promised his people. For Jews in Germany, life was terrible already. No one wanted Hitler to have another success, but at the same time another war looked like it could mean the end for everyone. On balance, the sacrifice of Czechoslovakia bought the Jews some time to emigrate. But what would have been the consequences if Hitler had not gotten his way?

The September crisis diverted everyone's attention from the departure of me and Licci and the inevitable day the family would break up. Soon the preparations resumed, and before one knew it, October 30, 1938 had arrived. Having brought up two children of my own, I can imagine the pain our parents must have suffered seeing their children leave within two days of each other, me for China and Licci for England the very next day. There did not seem to be much hope that the family would be reunited any time soon, particularly with me departing for the other side of the world. We were only allowed to take some clothing, the equivalent of $10.00 in currency, my gold watch and chain, (my bar mitzvah gift from my Grandparents Singer), and a specially made ring containing one ounce of gold. Somehow my chess set and stamp collection made it with me, too. I am happy that I still have my watch, ring, and chess set. I did eventually

Signet Ring containing One Ounce of Gold

need to sell the stamp collection. The temptations to sell personal items in times of need were great.

I have little recollection of our leave taking place at the railroad station on the morning of October 30, 1938 as I boarded the train for Trieste. It must have been so traumatic that I suppressed all memories of it. And my parents had to go through the same trauma again the next day when Licci left.

I think the excitement of the unknown repressed all feelings and fears, at least for a little while. The first exciting stop was the Austrian border. The Nazis could pull anyone off the train. You were not safe until the train had crossed the border into Italy. When we reached the Italian border, the Jewish people were taken off the train to be searched. We were taken into a room and had to take our shoes off so that they could be checked. I had only a small overnight suitcase. All of my other luggage had been shipped directly to the boat. In the suitcase, there was a box of chocolates for Miss Ellig. The border guards started to break a few pieces, presumably to look for hidden jewelry. Father also had given me a package of condoms and I distinctly remember standing there and wondering what would happen if they opened that package. It could have been unpleasant given the warped minds of these people. Thankfully, they did not open it, I got back on the train and the train continued on. When the Italian border guards came on board, I knew I was free of the Nazis. Free to do what? Who could know? But, at least for that moment, that's how it felt.

I did not sleep much that first night in the hotel alone in

Trieste and I have little recollection of how I got on board the ship the next day. My first memory is of arriving in Venice the next morning and going ashore. Venice, which I have visited twice since, made an indelible impression. It was a sunny day and the Piazza San Marco was something out of a dream. It was miraculous.

Venice – November 1938

The Italian liner *Conte Verde* was a ship of about twenty-five-thousand tons. Second class was quite luxurious in those days. The ship was on the Far Eastern run and served primarily the business community traveling to India and China. The cabin was rather small and I shared it with two middle-aged Englishmen traveling to Bombay. It was a stroke of luck that they disembarked in Bombay because I then had the cabin to myself for two-thirds of the trip. These two gentlemen proved very helpful. They let me buy cigarettes and other things for them with my "board money". The Nazis had permitted us to prepay the shipping line the equivalent of $100 to be used only aboard the ship. In that manner, I was able to acquire a few English pounds for future use.

Paul Aboard the Conte Verde

I met Bertha Ellig on board the ship. She was a tall, angular, rather mannish looking spinster in her fifties. As I mentioned earlier, it turned out that I had to look after her, more than she had to look after me. She got seasick as soon as the boat started moving, took to her bed, and as far as I can remember hardly ever made it to the deck. Bertha became a friend of the family and our need for each other's help was mutual.

There were many other refugees on board, names escape me now, but some of the people are very vivid in my mind. Most were very cordial to me, some ladies rather "motherly", some making their husbands jealous, although they really had no reason to be jealous. In retrospect, there may have been some missed opportunities, but I was too naïve to believe that it could be that easy.

The trip was pleasant, except for the continuous worry about the fate of my parents and my own future. The second night out after dinner, as we steamed out of Brindisi in southern Italy, it finally struck me that I had left Europe. Somehow everything had become irrevocable and suddenly I was very homesick. I went out to the deck alone and as I stood at the railing my eyes filled with tears. I am not one to cry easily. After awhile, I pulled myself together and went back into the lounge. This certainly was not my last attack of homesickness, but it was probably the worst because I remember it so vividly.

The highlights of the trip were the various stops. I clearly recall arriving in Aden in the evening. We had to go ashore in a small boat. The place looked like something out of "One Thousand and One Arabian Nights".

The next stop was Bombay. I have two very vivid memories of Bombay, a city of very wide boulevards. First, the guide took us to a cremation. In India this was, and probably still is, done on a funeral pyre. In my mind's eye, I can still see the turbaned corpse lying among the flames. Our next stop was at a Tower of Silence, where Parsis place their dead for excarnation, to be devoured by carrion birds. Thankfully, all we saw there were the circling vultures.

We had arrived in Bombay on November 10, 1938, one day after the infamous Kristallnacht, the Night of Broken Glass. The headlines in the papers spoke of the pogroms that had taken place in Germany and Austria on November 9, 1938. I immediately cabled home and was in agony for a week as more news about the horrors of that night appeared in the ship's paper. Finally, when the boat arrived in Singapore, I got a cable that my parents were safe. My parents did not know that they could radio the ship directly and had sent their cable to the shipping line's office in Singapore, which was two stops after Bombay.

My parents told me later on how they survived this terrible night. Probably the main event that saved them was the act of bravery by the concierge of our apartment building. She was a simple and devout woman. Whenever another group of Storm Troopers came looking for Jews she told them, "A bunch of your fellows were here awhile ago and you know how thorough your people are." She eventually was sent to a concentration camp for helping Jews. Our concierge was an example of a Righteous Gentile. She survived her imprisonment and I had the pleasure of visiting her when we were in Vienna in 1952.

There was another righteous person who helped my father that day. (Unfortunately, there were far too few of these individuals.) Father had to go out to see a patient. Father noticed that the taxi driver took him on a roundabout route, but at that moment did not understand why. Evidently the taxi driver knew what was going on, managed to avoid the road blocks and Father arrived home safely. One would have thought that Kristallnacht was enough to make everyone want to leave immediately, but it took another much more serious jolt eleven months later— deportation orders—for everyone to realize that time was up.

WITNESS TO HISTORY

Many passengers disembarked in Bombay and from then on the ship, particularly first and second class, was only about half-full. My memories of the next two stops, Colombo and Singapore, are blurred. I was very worried about the lack of news from home. Also, I visited these ports again in 1952, when we left Shanghai, and the later memories may have overshadowed what happened in 1938. Between Singapore and Manila, we ran into a typhoon. What an experience! The waves were crashing onto the deck. I was one of the three or four people who showed up for lunch. Eating was fun, particularly when a plate of soup started to slide towards you. Somehow, I managed not to be sick, just a little queasy. It was quite a feat since everyone else around me was hanging over the railing.

I don't remember much about our stops in Manila and Hong Kong, now probably because of the heightened anxiety about arrival in Shanghai. (I have also visited these ports of call again, both on our way out of China and on business, which may have further muddled my memory.) On the boat there were no worries. Food was served in abundance, entertainment was provided, and the only money needed was for food and alcohol. Alcohol was a minor consideration for me and I had plenty of board money for cigarettes. All this was about to change. After a four-week trip in relative luxury, I arrived in Shanghai, China on November 28, 1938, quite unprepared for what I would see and experience next.

9

SHANGHAI: GETTING SETTLED

WHO CAN forget the day of arrival in a new world?

It was a rainy and damp afternoon, already dark. There was commotion, noise, strange people and an indecipherable language. We were received by the Committee that had been organized to take care of the stream of refugees. I was among one of the earliest groups. Dr. Ehrlich was there to greet me and told me to come and see him the next day. We were put on buses to be taken to quarters arranged by the Jewish Refugee Committee. As we drove through the shadowy streets, we could see bombed-out houses, the remnants of the 1937 fighting between the Chinese and Japanese in Shanghai. As a result, the Japanese now controlled Hongkew, formerly a part of the International Settlement. The harbor was also in Hongkew, a part of town that would play an important role in the life of the refugee community, including my own.

The quarters assigned to me consisted of a very large room in a row of houses on Chusan Road. The other side of the street had been bombed and was nothing but ruins. There was electric light and there may have been running water, but I definitely know that there was no toilet, just a bucket. There was a young lawyer and his wife, the Sammetzes, who were assigned to the same house as me. When Mr. Sammetz saw the slop bucket, he

Hongkew Corner Photographed by Karl Heinz Praeger, Paul's future brother-in-law 1939

exclaimed, "I'd rather go into kidney failure than use this."

I am sure he learned to use the slop bucket, just like all of us. But I never got used to the absence of indoor plumbing, even though that was all that was available during the two-and-a-half years I eventually lived in Hongkew. Conditions were so eerie that the couple asked me to sleep in the same room with them. We went to bed without supper. There was no place to go and it certainly did not seem safe to go out. but as a matter of fact, it was very safe.

The next morning, the sun was shining and my first resolution upon waking up was not to spend another night in that room. Somehow, I had obtained some Chinese money and I went to a small establishment for breakfast a block away. The night before, I had been given instructions to return to the Committee offices. I took the trolley across the bridge to Museum Road in the International Settlement where the Committee was located. I met other refugees from the *Conte Verde* heading in the same direction.

PAUL HOFFMANN

Shanghai in 1938 consisted of the International Settlement, governed by the Shanghai Municipal Council, the French Concession governed by France, Hongkew under the control of the Japanese, all surrounded by large exclusively Chinese areas. The population, apart from millions of Chinese, consisted of at least 100,000 Japanese, which included the military, mostly living and stationed in Hongkew, and all other nationalities. Until the height of the refugee influx, the largest contingent of foreigners were about 20,000 White Russians, so called because they had fled from Red Russian Communist rule. A considerable number of British and Americans lived in Shanghai, large enough communities to have their own schools and clubs. Both the British and Americans had a small number of troops in the Settlement, as did the French in their part of town.

The Jewish population which was responsible for the Refugee Committee, consisted of a small closely-knit community of Middle Eastern Jews, mostly from Iraq and India. This community included the prominent Sassoon, Khadoori and Hardoon families. They had come to China in the 1800s as traders, including the opium trade, and were either British subjects or under British protection. Some, like the Sassoons and Kadooris, had become extremely wealthy. The Sassoons owned the power company, the transportation system and an enormous amount of real estate. The Khadooris owned the gas company.

The largest group of Jews in Shanghai was from Russia, a few thousand or so. Some had come to China before the Russian Revolution as business people, but most came after the Revolution. They were generally middle to upper middle class, store and restaurant owners. Many worked for English or American companies and banks. By 1938, a small group of Jews from Germany who had the foresight to leave Germany soon after Hitler came to power, had also settled in Shanghai. These three groups, with help from organizations from around the world, had formed the first relief committee to help the ever-increasing flood of refugees arriving with each boat from Europe. Even though I took no help from the Committee after that first day, the Committee performed marvelously for those who were in need of their assistance. Soon the problem of incoming refugees became too large for the resources the Committee could provide. By the time Pearl Harbor was attacked, some 20,000 to 25,000 refugees had arrived from Central Europe and more help had to be obtained from Jewish organizations overseas, primarily the United States.

My recollection as to what happened when I arrived at the Jewish Refugee Committee Offices on Museum Road is as follows: We were each given a sum of money, maybe the equivalent of US$10, told where to live, meaning the place we were the night before, and probably other important information, which I have now totally forgotten. What I do remember, is that from there I went to the Ossins. The Ossins, or Ossinovskys, as they were called in Russian, became, without question, the most important and most helpful people during the first year of my life in Shanghai. It is difficult to express how wonderful they were and how much they helped me. I am not referring to material things, although I ate many meals there, but by providing an anchor, a home away from home. The family consisted of Joseph, Sara, their daughter Nadja, who was about five years old at the time. Nadja was soon joined by a little brother, Ari, in 1941. Dr. and Mrs. Ehrlich and their daughter, Nadja, who was six years old, were also part of the household.

Mr. Ossin had American citizenship. He had been sent to college in the United States. Sara was twenty-eight and Joseph was about ten years older. She was very attractive, not beautiful but incredibly charming and always smiling, if not laughing, and

PAUL HOFFMANN

Paul with Mrs. Ossin and Nadja in Jessfield Park – April 1939

always kind. I cannot remember ever seeing her angry. I had a crush on her and she was a natural flirt. As a matter of fact, when I visited her in June of 1990 in San Francisco, she had not changed. She had just turned eighty, but her voice and lilting laugh were still the same. We reminisced and it was quite clear, that she had enjoyed all the attention she had received in Shanghai, and that she had liked me as well. She said, "You were the best looking boy of all the refugees who came to visit." I was a boy to her, and I think I understood that very well, because it was not long before I had girlfriends. Mr. Ossin also was a benevolent person, although it did not always appear so. He had to put up with all the comings and goings in his household and the attention being paid to his wife. I was very fond of Mr. Ossin, but only fully appreciated what he did and how he conducted himself as I matured.

True to my word, I refused to go back to Hongkew where I had spent the first night. I slept at the Ossins. Their apartment house was in the French Concession, which in our terms can probably best be described as a garden apartment. It had modern conveniences. I think I slept on a mattress on the floor. Two other fellows from the *Conte Verde* showed up, both several years older than I. I do not remember whether I gave them the address or if they had an introduction through someone else. All three of us stayed the night at the Ossins and the next morning set out to find a room. I remember only the name of one of them, Robert Ringel, a musician, who thought he could sing. Robert was rather short, nearly bald and went completely nuts over Sara. All I remember about the other fellow was that he was a more solid citizen than Robert. We found a room over a bar, with three beds, two blocks away from the Ossins. Most importantly, it had a water closet and it was in the French Concession, with the trolley right in front of the bar, on the corner of Avenue Joffre. I think the other rooms above the bar were let out to ladies of easy virtue. This did not matter to us. We had a place to stay in an area where many foreigners lived that was an enormous improvement over the first night's quarters.

I went back to Hongkew to get my luggage which, amazingly, was all there. I am sure I was much too trusting. I can't remember how I got the luggage five miles or so to my new quarters, but I know I did not take a rickshaw. Like all foreigners who first came to China, I was terribly shocked by a person pulling another human being in a little two-wheeled carriage, most of the time at a trot. Anyway, my luggage arrived and my new life began.

There was not much going on in Shanghai during the month of December due to the holidays. I spent the time getting acquainted with the city. It was a sprawling place, but for quite a while my explorations were limited to the International Settlement and the French Concession. Both were served by a very good transportation system consisting of trolley cars and buses. My first sight of double-decker buses was in Shanghai. There were rickshaws by the thousands, bicycles and a few cars. The cars were owned by the rich foreigners, mostly Americans and British, and rich Chinese. It was not customary for foreigners to walk, or for that matter, to take the bus or trolley. Whenever you stepped out of the house, a swarm of rickshaw coolies would surround you. Language was not as much of a problem as one would have thought. All languages were spoken in Shanghai. In the areas where foreigners lived, street signs were either in English or French and in Chinese. Many shop signs also were in other foreign languages. The Chinese people one dealt with on a daily basis had at least some English and one quickly learned to use Pidgin English. The Chinese are very good at learning languages and Chinese workers in Russian businesses or households quickly picked up some Russian. On the other hand, it is nearly impossible to learn Chinese by absorbing it, as is possible with other languages. The biggest obstacle is that one cannot read signs, or anything else, without having studied Chinese. In other languages with a common alphabet it is not difficult to read signs, and thus, as a beginning, learn a few words. I had English lessons in Vienna for four months at the most and somehow seemed to pick it up fairly easily. I had to speak English on the boat and as soon as I arrived in Shanghai. The Ossins spoke no German and I spoke no Russian. I remember Sara always correcting me. I also read the English newspaper and always carried a dictionary with me.

One vivid memory of these first days is being invited by the Ossins to go out with them on Christmas Eve. In accordance with the English customs that were dominant in Shanghai, Christmas Eve was not a religious holiday. We went to a nightclub. I was required to wear my dinner jacket. This was not the first time I had worn it. A dinner jacket was considered an essential article of clothing for a young man during this era and it was among the clothing that I brought from Vienna. I had the opportunity to wear it several times on the boat, but needed to ask the steward to tie my bow tie. By the time I arrived in Shanghai, I could do it myself. I danced with Sara at the party and had a wonderful time. I was also invited to a New Year's Eve gathering. Some fool at the party tricked me into drinking absinthe. After that I remember very little, other than I knew I would never touch the stuff again.

A question I have been asked is, "How does an eighteen-year-old, uprooted and transported into a totally foreign culture establish himself?" Somehow, it happened and I can recount some of the events, albeit not as many as I would like. I had a little money, a few dollars exchanged against my board money on the ship, the ten dollars I was permitted to take out of Vienna, the money the Committee had given me, and within a few days of my arrival I received a letter from my sister, Licci, containing a British five-pound note. That was quite a lot of money in 1938, at least enough to purchase food for a month. When asked, before leaving Vienna, what I would do to earn a living, I had said that all I really knew was what I had learned in school, and that is how I would earn money, by using what I knew. That was quite prophetic, because that is exactly what happened. I started tutoring shortly after the New Year in January of 1939. As I mentioned earlier, I tried to put my knitting machine knowledge to use. Somebody with a small factory gave me a chance. I lasted less than two days and that was forever the end of my career as a factory worker.

Shortly after the New Year, I got my first tutoring job. I am not sure whether I found my students through the Committee, by advertisement or by word-of-mouth. My first two pupils were two German brothers who went to the German school. Their

PAUL HOFFMANN

Paul tutoring circa 1940

father, Mr. Findorff, a businessman, did not approve of the Nazis and wanted to help refugees. But this was not purely a case of charity. These two boys needed tutoring. The brothers were about sixteen and fourteen-years-old and I would go to their house after their school day. Ironically, they were members of the Hitler Youth, which had a branch in Shanghai. It would have been unthinkable for me, a Jew, to teach Aryan boys in Vienna. In Vienna, they would not have even spoken to me, much less received instruction. But in Shanghai, they gave me no trouble. Their Papa wanted them to do well in school and made sure that they were well-behaved. Eventually, they had to return to Germany, where they probably died for their Führer.

Other pupils followed. First there was another German boy whose name was Erdman. There was no father on the scene and his mother was always very nice to me. Only later did I figure out that she may have had an ulterior motive. She was not the only lonely mother who liked the young tutor. I started to get pupils from the American School and my career for the next seven years was established. Miss Ellig, my friend from the boat, asked me to teach her English. While she certainly needed to learn English, I am sure she also was trying to help me out. If I ever earned my money, it was with her. Through her English sister-in-law, I met two spinster sisters who wanted to learn bridge and I took that on as well. Again, I suspect the motive was to help me, but this was another assignment that required patience and perseverance.

Sometime during the spring of 1939, I got a job as an advertising salesman for an American radio station in Shanghai, XMHA, "The Call of the Orient", managed by Roy Healy. I don't remember the circumstances that brought me to apply, but my English must have been quite good by this time in order to get the job. Once again, the fact that I was a refugee must have worked in my favor. People continually were coming to our aid. The newscaster at the station, Carol Alcott, had become well-known in the United States as a result of his broadcasts on the Sino-Japanese War. The broadcasts were pro-Chinese and very anti-Japanese. The United States supported the Chinese both politically and with armaments, including "volunteer" units, such as the Flying Tigers under General Claire Chennault. Naturally, relations between the Japanese and Americans were very strained. There were kidnappings and murders, primarily perpetrated by the Japanese. After the War, when I joined the law firm Allman, Kops and Lee, I learned that in 1937, Judge Allman had taken the post of Editor-in-Chief of the Shun Pao, the leading Chinese-language newspaper in Shanghai, to protect the Chinese editor, J.K. Shih. Shih was in grave danger from the Japanese due to the anti-Japanese sentiments of the paper. It was assumed that the Japanese would think twice before murdering a prominent American citizen such as Judge Allman. (There is a lot more to tell about Judge Allman and his extraordinary personal courage later.) To protect Alcott and the other station personnel, a policeman was always on guard outside the station. In fact, every time I went to the station, there was the possibility of something happening, such as a bomb being thrown, which was a favorite Japanese way of eliminating enemies. Fortunately, car bombs were not in style in those days. Maybe cars were too rare and expensive to be used in that fashion. I think

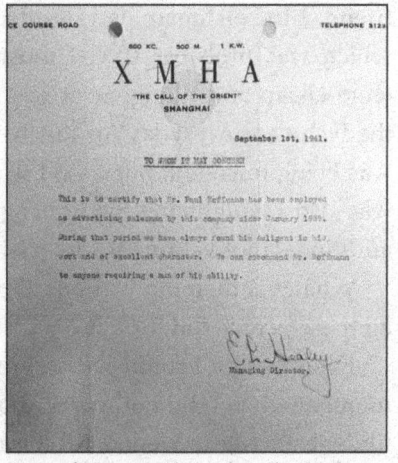

Letter of Recommendation from Roy Healey, Station Manager of XMHA

we became accustomed to the danger and learned to live with it without paying much attention on a daily basis.

Selling advertising was totally new to me. I had never done any kind of selling before. I found it very difficult to walk into a place and try to persuade people to buy something from me. The problem was even greater because I had nothing tangible to sell, just words spoken over the air. I remember going to fur stores, in one case not knowing that I was dealing with my future wife's uncle and that I would join the family eleven years later. Apparently, I did well enough, because when I quit in September 1941 to teach full-time, the station asked me to stay on for whatever time I could spare. I did not, but I had made friends with some customers and developed relationships that lasted for my entire stay in Shanghai.

In the spring of 1939, I contracted a very bad cold that led to bronchitis, which was not unusual for me. This time, I landed in the hospital. I am sure the Ossins arranged that I be taken there. When I came back home a few days later, Sara Ossin and her friend, Mrs. Fishman, had decided that I was undernourished, which was probably true. I mostly ate bananas because they were cheap and filling. So it was arranged that I would go to the Fishmans everyday for lunch, where sometimes it felt like I was being force-fed. But soon I was back on my feet. That there was also a daughter of the right age in the house may have been additional motivation for Mrs. Fishman, but I did not oblige.

Whatever their motivations, there is no way to diminish what all these people did for me.

Even though I could see progress for myself, there was not a moment when I did not worry about my parents, who were still under Nazi rule in Vienna. All communication was by mail which took at least two weeks. Letters traveled through Russia on the Trans-Siberian Railroad. There was no airmail and certainly no inter-continental telephone. If letters didn't arrive as expected, I worried. And while I always was a worrier, these worries were justified.

By May of 1939, I was financially able to take a small room for myself. It was high time. It was getting extremely difficult to live with the other two fellows for various reasons, including jealousy over relations with the Ossins. The fact that I was making more money than they, although I was much younger, certainly didn't help matters either. One time, we nearly came to blows.

My new little room was in a very pleasant neighborhood in the French Concession. Except for the Chinese people on the street, it looked like a European city. The only trouble with the room was that, like so many places in Shanghai, it was overrun by bedbugs. What a struggle it was to get rid of them! But I eventually won, at least partially.

Every boat brought a new load of refugees, among them my cousin, Erwin Lengyel, his wife Grete and their two children. Erwin and his family went to live in the town of Yu Yao, south of

Shanghai. He served as the only Caucasian doctor there for the duration of the War. Although we were separated for years at a time, an important relationship developed. Erwin was present when my son, Abe, was born in Vienna and when Father died in Utica, New York. Unfortunately, in his old age, Erwin has moved to Michigan to be close to his daughter and we are now rarely in contact.

That spring, I also had my first girlfriend in Shanghai, a girl named Hedi, but my heart was still with my last girlfriend in Vienna, Edith. It was quite a shock when I found out that Edith had gotten married in Czechoslovakia, where she had migrated to soon after the Nazis came to Vienna. What terrible tricks fate played in those incredible times! When Czechoslovakia was occupied by the Germans in March of 1939, Edith tried to escape to Israel. The transport was intercepted by the British, who in 1919 had been awarded a Mandate over Palestine by the League of Nations. The British were afraid of Arab reaction if they permitted Jews to enter Palestine freely. Edith ended up interned in Crete. When the Germans landed in Crete she disappeared, probably into a concentration camp. This is just one of the many tragic stories all of us who survived are able to tell.

I was also in regular correspondence with my sister, Licci, in England. She was doing okay, but did not like being a maid. About that time, I penned a letter to Licci saying that I thought it would be a good idea if she came to Shanghai. I remember very clearly writing that war would probably break out in Europe in late summer and that she might be in less danger in Shanghai than in England. I told her to leave England in late summer to avoid the very unpleasant weather in Shanghai. Also, I earned less money in summer since my pupils were on vacation. Our parents were all in favor of her coming to Shanghai, both because of the impending war and they wanted us to be together.

That first summer in Shanghai was a revelation. The heat and humidity were unbearable, particularly for someone coming from a moderate climate where temperatures of 90 degrees with 100 percent humidity were unknown. There was no air-conditioning. You perspired all the time, even when sitting or lying down, and little puddles would form under your elbows. Leather got moldy within a few days. Sleeping at night was particularly challenging. In the thirteen years I lived in Shanghai, I never got used to the summer. But I was young and started to play tennis, heat or no heat, went dancing and lived as normal a life as possible.

Another thing I could never get used to was watching the rickshaw coolies running in such weather, but maybe winter was even worse for these poor fellows. Nevertheless, like all foreigners, I learned to use a rickshaw. It soon became clear that not using the rickshaws did not help the coolie at all. He needed your fare, and as a foreigner you paid at least fifty percent more

Paul in Rickshaw 1940

than a Chinese person.

Great precautions had to be taken with water and food since dysentery and other digestive tract ailments were endemic and deadly. I can state with certainty that in the thirteen years I lived in China, I did not drink water that had not been boiled, fruit that had not been peeled or vegetables that had not been cooked. Salad was out of the question. Still, like most of the foreigners, I contracted amoebic dysentery, a most unpleasant and debilitating disease. I do not know what I ate when I contracted it, but no precaution could avoid a fly sitting on your food while you looked away. The greater part of town had no sewage system and the human waste was collected in the mornings, by what were euphemistically called honey carts, to be used by farmers as fertilizer. A sensitive nose was not an asset in China. Other smells were equally unpleasant; the smell of peanut oil, widely used by the Chinese both in and out-doors, is not easily forgotten. Given the unhygienic conditions, other illnesses such as malaria, typhus, typhoid fever and cholera, just to name a few, were rampant. One had to get yearly vaccinations, which were rather painful, but if you contracted any of these diseases it was a matter of life and death, and more often death in those days before penicillin and antibiotics.

Now that I was settled in Shanghai, it became increasingly clear that time was growing short for the rest of the family in Europe.

10

War Breaks Out

The summer of 1939 saw the war clouds thickening and it became quite clear that war in Europe was imminent. Hitler made ever-increasing demands, now directed at Poland. The Western Allies, primarily England and France, simply could not afford another Munich Agreement, which allowed for the annexation of the Sudetenland, and remain viable powers. The effect of the outbreak of war on our family could not be foreseen, but one thing was certain, my parents in Vienna were in great danger. Licci was to embark on a French ship going to Shanghai in late August. I was very happy to hear she was coming to Shanghai and made preparations for her arrival, primarily by renting a much bigger room. I remember it well. It was on Avenue Haig in the French Concession. I was somewhat naive in what I expected life would be like, having my sister with me, but I will explain a little later how this would prove to be just another one of life's challenges.

Every boat brought more refugees from Central Europe, and the Japanese started to worry about all these foreigners arriving. I do not know whether they were prodded by the Germans or worried about potential enemies, since all these people had to be presumed hostile to the Axis powers, the alliance of Germany, Italy and Japan. It is even conceivable that some Chinese leaders complained to the Japanese authorities about the large influx of refugees. The Japanese answer was to require that every refugee present a landing permit upon disembarking. This was easily enforced since the Japanese controlled the harbor and all railroad stations. In order to get a permit, one had to prove that the refugee had a job waiting for him or her in Shanghai. Thinking back, I am still astonished how quickly I reacted in trying to get a permit for my parents. After all, I was not yet nineteen years old. I had met the head of the Jewish hospital in Shanghai, Dr. Steinman, and asked him to give me a statement that my father would be employed by the hospital upon his arrival. It was not easy to convince him that I would guarantee that Father would not claim the job or make any demands upon him, or the hospital. It took several visits and a lot of begging and pleading, but he eventually relented, accepting my written promise that what I had said was true. I do not remember whether I got permit number one, but its number was certainly in single digits.

As it turned out, my very prompt action probably saved my parents' lives. All these years later, I consider this the most important thing I ever did. As my secretaries used to say, I always wanted everything done yesterday. Maybe this particular event laid the foundation for this stance throughout my life.

When the infamous and ignoble Hitler-Stalin pact was announced, war had become inevitable and broke out on September 1, 1939. Now Licci's fate became my main concern. She had embarked on a French boat at the end of August, and for several weeks I did not know where she was. The French would not give out any information about the location of the ship for fear of German spies, nor did the manifest distinguish between German Nationals and German Jewish refugees. Finally, the boat arrived in Shanghai early in October and Licci was on it. It is not easy to describe the emotion that goes with waiting at the landing, not knowing whether your sister would be on the arriving boat. Licci and all the other refugees had been under arrest. They were put into steerage and were constantly threatened with disembarkation in a French colony, such as Indochina, to be kept there for the duration of the War. Her first words to me were, "I am hungry". This probably characterizes best how the French behaved during the War. Their treatment of Jews in France was equally shameful.

I had great hopes of how nice it would be to have Licci with me. Our relationship in Vienna, particularly during the very difficult months from the arrival of the Nazis to our emigration had been fine, but things didn't turn out well when she arrived in Shanghai. Probably the biggest problem was Freddy, the fellow she met on the boat, and apparently had fallen in love with. Freddy seemed to think that I should not only take care of my sister, but him as well. It just didn't sit very well with me to come home from a day's work and have him around every day eating our food. He never offered to contribute anything or seemed to be looking for work. Was I jealous of the attention he paid my sister? I don't think so. In my role as man of the house, I had to support them and did not want to be treated like a nuisance that disturbed them. Anyway, this caused a lot of friction, and probably would have led to a serious break if our parents hadn't arrived. They totally agreed with my assessment of Freddy, and soon thereafter, Licci dropped Freddy for one of his friends, Karl Heinz Praeger, a refugee from Berlin. Heinz had been among the young Jewish men who were rounded up on Kristallnacht and was imprisoned for three months in the Dachau Concentration Camp near Munich. Heinz's father paid for his release from the camp, which was possible at the beginning of the War. One of the conditions of the release was that Heinz would leave Germany immediately. Two weeks later Heinz was on a boat to Shanghai.

Shortly after Licci arrived, it was still October, we got a telegram from our parents saying they had been ordered to appear one week later at the Gestapo offices, the infamous police arm of the Nazis, with one suitcase for transport to a camp.[5] Today we know what this meant; almost certain death. Even though it was not yet known that these camps were actually extermination camps, it was most frightening to leave everything behind and be shipped off to Poland. I can only guess that Father was called early on because the Nazis wanted doctors when setting up the camps. It seems contrary to what actually happened in the camps, but who can understand the thinking or intentions of these criminals.

Fortunately, with equal perversity, the Nazis made exceptions for Jews who had served in the First World War, and in particular decorated soldiers. Due to the medals Father received, my parents were granted an extension of two months. If they could show documentation of a place to go, they could leave Vienna. This meant they needed an entry visa and a ticket to somewhere in the world. This is where the landing permits I had obtained became important. The next hurdle was to get boat tickets. Italy had not yet entered the War and tickets were available on the same Italian boat on which I had traveled, the *Conte Verde*. The Nazis insisted that one ticket be paid in US dollars. Yet, it was forbidden to have US dollars. The Germans were trying to accumulate as much foreign currency as possible for their war effort. Licci and I did not have the few hundred dollars that were needed. As a matter of fact, it was beyond our wildest hopes to raise that amount of money. I tried to borrow from various people without success. Licci had been able to take Mother's diamond ring with her when she left Vienna and I went to plead

---

5   See Appendix: Deportation Order (Original 1 & 2) Oct 19, 1939, Deportation Order (Translation) Oct 19, 1939

with Mrs. Kahn, the wife of a rich Jewish banker who had come to Shanghai in the 1920s. I offered to leave the ring as security, but all I got was maybe, not a sufficient promise given the deadline we faced. I am not sure why we didn't try to sell the ring and other jewelry. I think that all this begging and pleading left a mark on me and made me even more determined never to have to plead for help again. Fortunately, Uncle Richard, who was in Boston, came to the rescue by providing the dollars for the one ticket, and by January 1940 the family was reunited. Only in retrospect, having learned what happened to so many other families, can one appreciate how lucky we were to have escaped and to be together.

I was doing rather well with my tutoring and my sales job, but my responsibilities had increased greatly. I was now the main breadwinner for a family of four. Eventually, Licci was able to help out and very occasionally Father brought in some income, but the main burden was mine at the age of nineteen. At first, I had rented two rooms in the French Concession, but a year or so later we moved to the Western district, to a small apartment, the upper floor of a two-family house owned by Chinese people who occupied the ground floor. The main problem was that our landlord loved to play his Chinese fiddle every afternoon after lunch, emitting sounds comparable to a screeching owl or a howling cat, depending on the song played. Licci and I shared a small room and our parents had the larger room, which also served as a living room. We also had a balcony, kitchen facilities and a bathroom. I can still see the place in my mind.

Father opened an office in town and very slowly acquired some patients. Understandably, he suffered most from the changes in our lives. I have often wondered how I would have conducted myself if at the age of fifty-two, if I suddenly found myself totally uprooted and thrust into a completely alien culture. How do I describe the culture shock between central Europe and China? The contrast between Vienna and Shanghai was stark. Language, food, culture, and climate, everything was different. And, how does one cope with the loss of one's friends and family? I think we all proved that humans are exceptionally adaptable creatures.

In September of 1940, Father decided that he needed a prostate operation. I have often wondered how necessary it really was, given his age and the psychological impact of this surgery. It is possible he hoped he would not survive, and he nearly didn't. It was touch-and-go for a while, in part due to the incompetence of the surgeon. The morning after the surgery, I came to the hospital to find Father bleeding and complaining about how rough the surgeon had been. I fired the surgeon on the spot and found another refugee doctor in the hospital. I was quickly told my blood was needed for a transfusion. Medical technology was nothing compared to today, but Father survived. In due course this crisis passed and by my twentieth birthday in October 1940, life seemed more or less to have settled down.

The year 1940 was difficult, but bearable for the Hoffmanns. The War news was terrible. There were the defeats of France, and Dunkirk. The fall of Paris was particularly traumatic. Every German victory increased our fear, not only for ourselves, but for all the Jews in Europe, a fear that unfortunately proved justified in the end. I was able to get a landing permit for my Aunt Margit, my mother's older sister, and her husband Edmund. They managed to come to Shanghai in June of 1940. As mentioned earlier, mother's oldest sister, Stephanie, and her husband declined to come to Shanghai. My father's oldest brother, Eduard, and his wife, did not accept my parents' offer to take their fifteen-year-old daughter with them to Shanghai. I shudder to think what happened to my aunts and uncles and especially this beautiful young girl.

The next date which I have well engraved in my mind is a Sunday in mid-June 1941 when the news that Germany had attacked Russia came over the radio, just as I was leaving to play tennis. I was happy about the German attack because I believed, quite correctly as it turned out, that Hitler had made the same mistake as Napoleon when he invaded Russia in 1812. Little did I know that it would lead to the murder of millions of Jews, as well as many others. I have always been amazed how leaders cannot see the consequences of an act that an ordinary person, with only a reasonable knowledge of history, can foretell. True the first news from the War continued to be bad, but it became evermore evident that Hitler could not continue to fight on many different fronts and soon the first reports of Allied victories started coming from North Africa.

The fact that I was playing tennis, shows how life goes on, no matter what, and that our family was breathing a little easier. We were not alone; the refugee community showed enormous resilience despite the incredible difficulties it faced.

I played tennis at the Jewish Club, which like other foreign clubs used the infield of the Shanghai Race Course, only about a mile from downtown. Unbelievably, Chinese people were not allowed into the Race Course except during race days, and were restricted to certain areas. They could serve as ball boys or in other menial jobs, but could not use the facilities, or even have their own club. The belief was that if the Chinese would be permitted in, they would overrun the place; true, but this was their country. This was really not racial, because the Indians had their own cricket club. Was I disturbed by the obvious injustice? I don't think so at the time. This was part of life in China and one accepted the situation and enjoyed the conveniences and privileges.

The next few months again brought some big changes in my life. There were never more than a few months between each new upheaval during those years. During the summer of 1941, the tensions between the United States and Japan increased steadily, primarily because the United States placed an oil embargo on Japan and increased its support for China. American citizens were urged to leave China and many did, particularly women and children. This led to the closure of the Shanghai American School. However, there were enough pupils of all nationalities, including Americans, to warrant the continuation of a school. Frank Cheney, a teacher at the school, undertook to organize the American Private School and offered me a job as an algebra and geometry teacher. I later also took over chemistry and physics, which required a great deal of chutzpah, since these were not my strongest subjects; contrary to mathematics, which was my strength.

So at the age of twenty-one, I started teaching high school in English, a language I had just learned. I believe Mr. Cheney offered me the job because I had tutored a number of youngsters from the Shanghai American School and had become well-known in the community. Apparently, a number of parents had shared that I was competent and got results, which was not always easy, since the brightest and most diligent students were not the ones in need of private tutoring.

Mr. Cheney, known to all as "Unk", was a teacher at the Shanghai American School, and did not want to go back to the States. He had been in Shanghai for many years. Unk was about fifty years old and apparently did not see any future for himself in the States. He was a real gentleman, always kind, but also firm. Unk really cared for and loved his pupils and in turn he was liked and well-respected. He had taken in a Jewish refugee boy, Jimmy, who I believe he adopted. I really knew nothing of

Unk's background so it was all speculation as to why he did not want to return home. The Japanese ended up sending him to an internment camp for two years because he was an American.

For me, getting this job was an enormous step forward. Financially, I was doing really well since I was able to give private lessons in the afternoon in addition to a generous salary from the school. As soon as school started, I quit my job at the radio station. As it turned out, the job would not have lasted much longer. The station suspended operations the day war broke out.

11

Pearl Harbor

ONCE AGAIN, the "better" times did not last long. I had been at the American School barely three months when the Japanese attack on Pearl Harbor threatened to jeopardize all the gains we had made. I vividly remember Mother's forty-third birthday party on Sunday, December 7, 1941. My Aunt Margit and Uncle Edmund, Licci, Heinz, who by that time was Licci's boyfriend, were at our apartment. Licci and Heinz were going to a dance at the Jewish Club that night. Because of the time difference, Shanghai's Pearl Harbor did not happen until early Monday morning, about 3 AM local time.

When I woke Father the morning of December 8, 1941 to tell him the news, he said, "I told you so yesterday," and he had. We had discussed the seriousness of the situation the previous afternoon. It is hard to believe that what many of us in Shanghai guessed would happen, not necessarily the direct attack on Pearl Harbor, but that the outbreak of war in the Pacific was imminent, was not taken seriously enough in the United States.

(I know of one other incredible example of what was obvious to the general public but not heeded by those in power. At the beginning of the Korean War, Chinese troops were openly marching through the streets of Shanghai and when people asked where they were going, they responded that they were going to

Korea. Yet, General MacArthur testified before Congress that he was surprised when the Chinese crossed the Yalu River. I think leaders are sometimes so blinded by their own importance, and the "yes men" surrounding them, that they cannot see what is happening before their very own eyes.)

A Japanese cruiser was anchored in the Whangpoo River. The river flows through the center of Shanghai and the cruiser had been in front of the Japanese Consulate for quite some time. There was also a British gunboat in front of the British Consulate and an American gunboat, the *USS Wake*, tied up to a pier. About three o'clock on Monday morning, the Japanese cruiser fired shots across the bows of the two gunboats and demanded their surrender. The American captain took the sensible approach and complied, but the British captain refused, returned fire, and the boat was sunk. Of the twenty-two British crew members on board, six were killed. We heard all this Monday morning on the radio, but there were no other disturbances in the city. As a matter of fact, I decided to go to school. At the time, I shared a private rickshaw with Bertha Ellig. I used a fixed rickshaw in the morning to go to school. The rickshaw man was happy to serve us because he had a steady weekly income and we avoided the hassle of bargaining every day with different coolies. Even more importantly, we had a clean rickshaw in good repair. It was like having your own carriage, except, of course, it was pulled by a person. By this time, I must admit that I had become somewhat accepting of this form of transportation, and the coolie was much better off because he didn't have to roam the street searching for fares. I am sure he moonlighted for extra money whenever he was not needed by myself or Bertha, and that was fine with us.

My rickshaw came to pick me up on time on the morning of December 8, 1941. So, off I went. There were some barriers up in the streets, but I have no recollection of any kind of hassle passing through them. Most of the pupils showed up and Unk Cheney took the correct, and sensible, position that we should continue as if nothing had happened while awaiting developments. This is a lesson well-learned. When a situation is really serious, don't panic. Nothing will cloud your judgment more than panic. He was right. We were able to keep the school open until April 1943.

Life changed, but slowly, particularly for us, since we were not enemy nationals, like the Americans, British and Dutch. They were considered the three most important enemy groups in Shanghai, as far as the Japanese were concerned. Enemy nationals immediately lost their businesses. They had to wear armbands to indicate their nationality and some of the more prominent members were arrested, but most were eventually allowed to go free.

Life during 1942 was reasonably bearable as far as living conditions were concerned. I still had my job and some private lessons. Sometime in 1942, Father had to leave his office downtown and moved into an office uptown. There were just

Heinz and Licci wedding picture – Lili and Oskar in the background – October 1942

Heinz & Licci's 92 Tangshan Rd Apartment in Hongkew in 2019

a few patients, but it was important for his morale to have an office. I suspect that many months I had to subsidize the rent. I do not remember whether Licci was working, but more importantly, she and Heinz became engaged. On October 11, 1942 Licci and Heinz were married in what, unfortunately, had to be a very modest affair. They moved to Hongkew, where Heinz had been living since his arrival in Shanghai.

The war news was terrible. The fall of the Philippines and Singapore was preceded by the sinking of two big British battleships, and then the Dutch East Indies fell. It looked as if the Japanese could not be stopped. In the European Theater, the German advances in North Africa and Russia added to our fears. Since nearly all our news came from the enemy camp, it sounded even worse than it was. The only Allied news source was Russian broadcasts. These broadcasts did not give the impression of dependability since they were emanating from a dictatorship. By the second half of the year, the tide seemed to be turning, and then the Russian winter started to do its job. By the end of the year, the German defeat at Stalingrad was imminent and our spirits lifted a bit.

The silver lining of the reversal of fortunes for the Allies had its consequences for the refugee community. As the War turned against the Japanese, they became tougher on enemy nationals and in the middle of 1942 promulgated a decree affecting the

Jewish refugees. It is not entirely clear how this came about. The most believable explanation is that the Germans had sent Gestapo agents to Japan to convince the Japanese that the Jews also were their enemies. It was rumored, and I have little doubt that it was very close to the truth, that the Germans wanted the Japanese to exterminate all Jews, or as a minimum put them into German-style concentration camps, with the ultimate goal of extermination. The Japanese refused. The book *Japanese, Nazis and Jews* by Dr. David Kranzler is in my view the best and most reliable source to explain what actually happened. Dr. Kranzler postulates that the Japanese believed the Jews were powerful enough in the United States to influence the United States Government in its attitude towards the Japanese, should the Japanese need help if they lost the War. This belief was based in part on the financial help the Japanese had received from Jewish bankers, particularly the Schiff family, during the Russo-Japanese War of 1905. The help the Schiffs provided was motivated by hatred and anger sparked by Russian antisemetism and the resulting pogroms. According to Kranzler, the Japanese remembered with respect, and some gratitude, the financial contributions the Schiffs made to their war effort. Knowing how the Japanese operated, this theory is quite plausible. Given the way the Japanese treated the Chinese and other people in the countries they occupied, one cannot believe that they were motivated by any kind of humanistic impulse. Like everywhere else, there were some good and decent Japanese people, but not among those making the decisions in regard to the refugees at this time.

To satisfy the Germans, a ghetto was set up for the Jewish refugees that had arrived in Shanghai after December 31, 1937 and the Japanese promised more drastic steps in due time. That date had the effect of excluding the Russian and Sephardic Jewish communities that were well-settled in Shanghai. There were rumors that these groups were able to bribe the Japanese in decision-making positions to obtain this exemption. This may be true. A more charitable explanation may be that the leaders of the Russian Jewish community, which was the largest group concerned, was able to convince the Japanese that they could be useful to them in relations with the West. The Japanese, with their penchant for always leaving a door opened, agreed. Probably both the theories of persuasion and bribery have an element of truth.

Heinz's Pass Allowing Him to leave the Hongkew Ghetto-November/December 1944

The decree went out that by a certain date all refugees from Central Europe who had arrived in Shanghai after December 31, 1937 had to move to an area of Hongkew, which was not more than one square mile. The area was most likely chosen because most of the refugees already lived there. It was also one of the least desirable areas of the city. The decree stipulated that no one could leave the area without a pass from the Japanese police, or the gendarmerie as they were called. At the places where one could leave the ghetto, guards, mostly made up of refugees who had to serve on a rotating basis, were stationed to check passes. Spot checks were made outside the Ghetto; not a difficult task since a Caucasian person stood out, and everyone had to have some form of identification.

My own experience with the Ghetto was delayed about a

year. Father, as a doctor, also received an extension. This was an indication of the Japanese ambivalence towards the whole project and the respect in Asian culture for the educated person. For us, this meant another year in relative comfort and not being caught in the rush to move, which was, of course, exploited by those who had rooms to rent in Hongkew. Just to rent a wretched room commanded a high price up-front. Chinese landlords were no greedier than some of the refugees who had been able to buy one of the miserable row houses in Hongkew. Licci and Heinz lived in one of these row houses. Mother, Father and I eventually ended up in one, but more about that later.

I continued to teach school and also gave some private lessons, making rather good money. One of my pupils at school was Bermen Tang. She asked me to give her private lessons in algebra. Her father was a Chinese general serving with Chiang Kai-shek. Her mother, I believe, was German, but I was never able to figure out her background. Bermen was very attractive. The Tangs were well off and lived rather near us in their own house. Berman clearly had developed a crush on me, and I had no trouble falling in love with her. Lessons lasted much longer than an hour and were usually broken up by Mama Tang at the right moment. She must have known what was going on, but let her daughter have her way up to a point. Nobody thought of the impropriety of giving private lessons to a pupil you taught in school, or to have your pupil as your girlfriend, although we were never able to go out together. Bermen really suffered from being of mixed race, as did so many Eurasians. In my opinion, this was of course wrong, but the Eurasians were not fully accepted by either group. Bermen told me she would only marry a Chinese man and not have children. She followed through on that promise, as I found out when I met her again in the 1960s. She lived in Washington, DC, had married a Chinese man,

American Private School Graduation April 1943-Berman Tang-Front row third from right

and did not have children. Interestingly, her younger brother had married an American girl in Chicago and went on to have children.

The American Private School had to close in April 1943. Bermen graduated and our move to Hongkew later in the year terminated our contacts. I believe Mrs. Tang and the children left Shanghai, most likely to avoid being interned with the enemy nationals by the Japanese, a step taken by the Japanese as it became clear that they were losing the War.

In the spring of 1943, I made one of the most important and best decisions of my life. I decided I had to obtain a university degree. There was no possibility of pursuing my dream to study medicine, because it was impossible to study medicine and support oneself, let alone a family. Since mathematics was my second love, I thought I should try to work towards becoming an actuary. I looked around for a course that would help me to accomplish this goal. Aurora University, a French Jesuit university, offered one course, financial mathematics, in its three-year curriculum of law and economics. It was a far cry from what I had in mind, and certainly not even close to preparing me for becoming an actuary, as I found out when we arrived in the United States.

The university was run by French Jesuit priests, who made up the majority of the faculty with a sprinkling of lay professors. For instance, the mathematics professor was the former Czech Ambassador to China who was stuck in Shanghai when Czechoslovakia was overrun by the Germans. The school was mostly for Chinese students, but a few foreign students were accepted. I had to take an entrance examination in French since all the courses would be in French. For the Chinese students, there were many courses in Chinese. I passed the entrance exam and started my university education in September of 1943, a little less than five years after I came to Shanghai. I started under the most difficult conditions and when I think back on these years I find it hard to believe that this was at all possible. Going to night school in the United States to achieve my law degree at Brooklyn Law School, with a wife and two young children eleven years later was a breeze in comparison. But I was twenty-three years old and determined.

Since I still had to make a living, I had to set up classes with those pupils from the American School who had not been interned by the Japanese, mostly Russian Jewish students, a few Chinese students and some other nationalities. This worked out quite well. I recall I had classes of four or five students and taught them mainly math and some science. These classes had to be coordinated with my classes at the University. Arrangements had to be made with the parents as to whose house would be used, methods of payment and the acquisition of teaching materials.

Just as I had all this organized and had started at the University, our extension ran out and we had to move to the Hongkew Ghetto.

12

THE GHETTO: 1943—1945

I NOW COME to one of the top three worst time periods of my life. The six months under Hitler undoubtedly was the worst time. It is hard to say which was worse when comparing the other two episodes: life in the Hongkew Ghetto or life under the Communist Regime from 1949-1952. Each one was horrible and difficult for different reasons. Both were also very dangerous in different ways. As I reflect back, the Ghetto may have been worse.

The move to Hongkew was a devastating blow. Our standard of living dropped dramatically. Also, the distance to the University and my tutoring lessons increased enormously, at least fourfold. The change that had the greatest impact on me was the inability to leave the Ghetto without a pass from the Japanese. They had set up a system whereby guards were stationed at all the important crossings. The guards, all refugees, were what the Japanese called with appropriate irony "our" self-defense system, Pao Chia. Just like the Nazis had forced Jews into collaborating with them, the Japanese had refugees watching refugees. A question arises. Was civil disobedience an option to defy these restrictions? I doubt that it was in this situation. We were too few in a sea of Chinese. There was no place to hide as a foreigner. I am sure attempts at resistance would have been brutally suppressed. In retrospect, it is quite clear that compliance was the correct choice because the community survived with rather minimum loss of life, although the population of the Ghetto suffered significant hardship due to poverty, living conditions and illness.

In order to apply for a pass, one had to go to the Japanese police station set up in the District, as the Ghetto became known. The officer in charge was a man named Sargent Kano Ghoya. Ghoya was the ultimate authority on whether or not passes were granted, as well as all other matters concerning the refugees. Most of us had little understanding of the Japanese character and were hard-pressed to figure out why Ghoya behaved the way he did. Here was a man who suddenly had been given more power over more people than he probably had ever dreamed of, and he was not at all reluctant to abuse his power. Ghoya denied passes on a whim, slapped people around and went into sudden rages. On other days, things went more smoothly and everyone got a pass without incident. There was no way of knowing whether you would be issued a pass on a particular day, even if a pass had been issued for the same reason several times before. You always had to line up early, which meant the middle of the night. You never knew how many passes Ghoya would decide to issue on any given day.

This process was so intolerable that Father, who had tried to keep up his office outside the Ghetto, gave up. He just could not withstand the humiliation and uncertainty, not to speak of the physical strain of waiting in line for hours. Unfortunately, it really did not matter financially that Father did not pursue leaving the Ghetto. There weren't enough patients to warrant the rent for the office; another psychological blow for Father. This left me as the sole supporter of the family, a role I had become used to over the years. I was never denied a pass. I don't recall how long passes were issued for, but in my case, because I was a student, it was probably for two months at a time. Imagine the anxiety I felt every time I waited on line. Denial of the pass would have meant an end to my studies and my income. I thought it best not reveal that I was tutoring, only that I was a student. I may have benefited from the Asian respect for learning and the emphasis on school. I could tell many stories about this horrid little man, who had the audacity to call himself the "King of the Jews" as he swaggered around the Ghetto, but I prefer to go on.

The Ghetto became a little city unto itself with its own newspapers, health facilities, stores, tradesmen and entertainment. This economic and social development was made possible, in part, by funds coming in from the United States through Switzerland to support those that could not support themselves. The Chinese people in the area participated in the economy, people like me brought money in from outside the Ghetto and many people sold what they had left, including jewelry, even wedding rings. I sold my stamp collection when things got tight. As always, there were some people who managed to do well, but the great majority lived hand to mouth.

When Mother, Father and I had to move to Hongkew, the only place we could afford was a room on the second floor in a building either owned or leased by the Jewish Relief Committee. The room was at most 12 feet by 15 feet, and had to serve as a bedroom, living room, kitchen, washroom and Father's office when somebody wanted to consult with him. Impossible as it seems, that is how we lived. Water had to be carried in and the cooking facility was just one hibachi, essentially a flower pot with charcoal. Toilet facilities consisted of a row of stalls with buckets on the ground floor for use by all the tenants, of which there were many.

It quickly became obvious that I could not stay in that room with my parents for any length of time. Since we still had a little money left, I was able to rent a room a few blocks away in a house owned by a refugee family who had bought it from Chinese proprietors and now rented out a few rooms. It was a typical Chinese row house in a lane. It had one tap with a small basin on the first floor landing and its toilet facility for all of us consisted of an outhouse with a bucket on the roof. The one window in my room overlooked the roof. No comment is necessary to describe the stench that emanated when the wind blew in the wrong direction or when the coolie came every morning to empty the bucket. The room was no more than 6 feet by 8 feet. There was just enough space for my bed and a desk. Even though I can still see the room and the house in my mind, I don't recall where I kept my clothes. When it rained, the only dry place was the bed. Since we had to observe a blackout every night and shades were drawn, the place was infernally hot in summer. I'm certain it had no heating. I just don't remember how I managed to keep warm when it got damp and cold in winter. If I needed light at night, I had a wick and peanut oil, and I did quite a bit of studying with the light it provided. As hard as it is to imagine this situation, necessity demanded it work. Did the place have anything by which to recommend it? Yes, it did. The young landlady, who was very fond of me, did her best to entertain me when her husband was not home. He was either working late in the bar they owned, or on the guard duty imposed on the refugees by the Japanese. Unfortunately, the walls were paper thin, which, to say the least, created all kinds of problems.

My sister Licci and her husband Heinz also had a very difficult time during the War. Heinz did not have the type of profession that enabled him to readily obtain a pass to leave the Ghetto. Heinz made some money with his photography among the refugees, but more often than not the Praegers had to rely on help from the Committee. Nevertheless, hope springs eternal

Jack and Opa Oskar – Spring 1946

and in February 1945 their son, Jack, was born. That it was difficult to take care of a baby under the prevailing sanitary and economic circumstances is an understatement. According to my recollection, Jack did not contract any of the serious illnesses that attacked so many other babies. He was everyone's joy. Father particularly doted on him and visited every day. Jack certainly was not the only baby born in the Ghetto under circumstances that would convince one it was more sensible to wait for better times to bring a child into the world. But who waits? I was no more practical when my wife, Shirley, became pregnant in 1951.

No matter how bad or difficult it was, life took on a certain routine. I had a very old bicycle which was prone to breaking down, but nevertheless attractive to thieves. It took vigilance to avoid it being stolen. Five days a week, I bicycled from the Ghetto to the French Concession where Aurora University and most of my private pupils were located. My guess is that I traveled about twenty miles each day, regardless of heat or rain. If the weather was really bad, trolley cars were available, but they were terribly crowded, and even less reliable than my poor bicycle. The biggest problem was getting back to the Ghetto on time. You had to leave some margin of error in order to arrive before curfew. Being caught outside the Ghetto after curfew by a Japanese patrol could have disastrous consequences. This happened to a few Polish students. While a sentence of a few days in jail does not seem particularly harsh, it was in fact a death sentence for five of the students. They contracted typhus in jail and died.

Did I break the rules? Yes. Once in a while, I slept over outside the Ghetto, being careful not to be on the streets after seven in the evening. It is not difficult to guess that a woman was involved on these evenings. Normally, I returned to the Ghetto in time for dinner in my parents' room and then went to my little cubicle with my peanut oil wick to study, which was not always easy. The distractions from the noise of people congregating outside, particularly in warm weather, made studying very difficult. On the weekends and summers, if there was any time left from studying and preparing lesson plans for my pupils, there were places to go dancing within the confines of the Ghetto with

Edmund, Margit, Oskar, Lili, Heinz and Licci-Seder 1946

friends. The social life in the Ghetto was surprisingly active. Family events and Jewish holidays were observed, although we did not go to a synagogue. The family consisted of our immediate family, my sister's husband, Heinz, and Aunt Margit and her husband, Edmund.

I was not spared having to serve guard duty. Because I was out during the day, my duty was usually in the middle of the night. We were equipped with a nightstick and an armband. I stood for three hours at a lonely corner where, because of curfew, there was no one on the street between 12 midnight and 3 AM. To this day I do not know what we were guarding and from whom. In my opinion, it was nothing more than another device by the Japanese to make life difficult. One day, I forgot to go on duty. Luckily, my punishment was very light; the gendarmerie just doubled my duty to six hours. I still remember spending those six hours at the corner where the incinerator was in the company of a male corpse, deposited there by relatives who could not afford a decent burial and expected the body to be burned with the trash. This was a fairly common occurrence.

The lack of reliable news on the progress of the war was another one of the unpleasant aspects of our life. Our best source was Russian news programs, which the Japanese had to permit since the two nations were not at war. People had shortwave radios and rumors ran amok. We did not hear anything about the horrible things that were happening to the Jews in Europe. Most of that information only came to light after the War, when people actually saw what had occurred in the camps. Before that, nobody would have believed that such unspeakable horrors could happen.

In 1944, the bombing started. The United States had advanced far enough to make it possible to bomb Shanghai. This may seem strange in a world with intercontinental ballistic missiles. The purpose was to destroy Japanese naval facilities in Shanghai, to harass the Japanese in general, and deliver encouragement to the Chinese people that their allies were coming. I remember three air raids. For two of these raids, I was at home. One was at night and I fell out of bed as a bomb exploded not too far away from my apartment. Another raid occurred on a Sunday morning. We had no shelters and stood outside in the narrow lane listening to the bombs explode. It was a very frightening experience. The worst raid occurred about six months before the end of the War. I distinctly remember seeing the planes flying high overhead at around noon while riding my bicycle in the French Concession. Upon returning to the Ghetto that night, I heard the grim news. A bomb had hit one of the refugee camps, killed a few and injured many. Apparently a Japanese depot of some sort was located in the vicinity and the inevitable accident happened. No one I knew was killed but the whole community felt the tragedy of people being killed by "friendly fire".

The Allied invasion of France was the good news of 1944. With the arrival of 1945, it was clear that the War in Europe would end soon and the defeat of the Japanese could not be far behind. The question was, could we survive to see it? Living conditions had deteriorated; almost everyone was sick with some kind of intestinal infection and money was running out, if it had not run out already. Nevertheless, we all continued in the routines of daily life as best we could.

May 8, 1945 was a red-letter day. Germany surrendered unconditionally. I remember it very well because Heinz and I got drunk celebrating. All we had to drink was rum and peppermint liqueur, and I haven't had either to drink since. While our hopes and spirits were greatly lifted by anticipating the end of the War, our living conditions did not improve at all. Also, we began to hear the first devastating news of the horrors committed by the

Germans and their henchman, particularly the Poles, Ukrainians and Croats.

I finished my second year at the University and continued to give private lessons. In late July of 1945, I contracted malaria and was very sick. This was in addition to the chronic amoebic dysentery, which stayed with me until 1954, after we came to the United States. I mention the malaria attack because the day the atomic bomb devastated Hiroshima, August 6, 1945, was my first day back to work after being sick.

I had come home early from having dinner with my parents totally exhausted. I was on my way to my room, but suddenly my apartment house was buzzing with the rumor that the Japanese had surrendered. I hopped on my bicycle and went back to my parents to share the good news with them. The rumors were equally thick there, but the overriding problem of the moment was that Father was also very sick. He had developed a high fever and diarrhea. By the next morning he had gone to the bathroom some forty times. Just imagine, each time he had to go to the bathroom, he had to go down and up a flight of stairs. By morning he had to be taken to the hospital. He had bacillary dysentery. Father had risked eating watermelon. The Chinese would put melons into the sewers to cool them and increase their weight, having put little pin holes in the melons so they could absorb the water from the sewer. Only the new sulfa drugs, which had just reached China from Switzerland, saved his life.

The rumors proved to be true. Three days later, after the second atomic attack on Nagasaki, the Japanese surrendered and the War was over.

13

Peace: 1945–1946

The end of the war brought incredible feelings of elation and hope. These feelings were tempered at first by the fear of potential retribution by the Japanese Army, or a Chinese mob that might engage in looting and all the other terrible things mobs might do. This did not happen, primarily due to the amazing discipline of the Japanese military.

The Japanese were told to keep order and they did. The Japanese soldiers were subjected to all kinds of physical attacks from those they had oppressed. The Japanese sentries were spat upon and rolled along the pavement. They did not retaliate. There were Japanese soldiers billeted in a building where a German acquaintance of mine lived who owned a radio. The soldiers were taken to the apartment to listen to Emperor Hirohito's speech announcing the Japanese surrender. My friend told me how stoically they listened, without any outward sign of emotion, and quietly filed out after the speech.

On the first or second day of peace, I rode my bicycle to the internment camp where enemy civilians had been imprisoned by the Japanese. As soon as the inmates had heard the news of the surrender, they arrested the commandant and his soldiers and took over the operation of the camp. Again, it was remarkable how the Japanese, after all the atrocities they had committed, quietly accepted orders. I met many of my friends in the camp, including our headmaster at the American School, Mr. Cheney. He had already decided to reopen the American Private School as soon as possible. Everyone told me about the hardships; the hunger and deprivations of the camp. I also heard about the harsh rule by the Japanese and the poor behavior of some of the inmates. I wonder what was worse, the Ghetto with its very limited freedom and the difficulties of feeding yourself, or the camp with its protection, albeit very limited under international law. On balance it probably was a wash.

The first few days after the liberation were a heady experience. No more barriers at the Ghetto, no more passes, no more sentries at the bridges. There really was no authority in Shanghai. The Chinese and Allied troops were close to a thousand miles away. Allied warships were also many days away. The surrender caused by the atom bombs had come too quickly to make preparations for liberation and occupation.

I know there are to this day people who decry the atrocity of unleashing the bombs on Japan. I am convinced those who have these sentiments have never experienced what it feels to be at the end of your physical and psychological resources, and then the relief of being liberated. I am convinced that the atomic bombs used on Hiroshima and Nagasaki saved hundreds of thousands of lives, including the Japanese who would have died either in the field or as civilians if the War had lasted only a few months longer. The same discipline that made the Japanese surrender quietly when told to do so, would have made them fight against all odds. They would have conducted themselves like the Germans who continued their war effort and, in the process, killed tens of thousands long after the War was clearly lost. As true as it is that the bombs killed people that otherwise might not have been killed, overall, fewer people died. It is also clear to me that the demonstrated horror which atomic bombs can inflict has limited the wars over the subsequent years and brought relative peace to the world. From a personal point of view these arguments are superfluous. I am not sure I would be here to tell this story if the War had lasted much longer.

I must recount the events of the "official" liberation of Shanghai. A few days after the Japanese surrender, an American lieutenant and five soldiers were flown into Shanghai. Lieutenant Kim was a Korean-American. I knew his family because I had taught his brother at the American School. Upon arrival, Lieutenant Kim and his entourage had no sanctioned place to go, so they went to the Swiss Consulate. Somehow, I had been informed of their arrival and I was there with a small crowd to welcome them. These six American soldiers appeared on the balcony of the Consulate and that in effect was the entirety of the liberation of Shanghai by the Allied armies. One lieutenant and five soldiers; hard to believe, but I witnessed it. Again, it speaks volumes for the Asian character that all this occurred peacefully, without any disturbances.

As time went by, Chinese troops and their American liaison personnel entered the city. The Allied ships, mostly American and some British, sailed into the harbor. Needless to say, the sailors, primarily the Americans, dominated the landscape. They had money, nylons, chocolates, cigarettes, and they attracted the girls and women of all nationalities. It still amazes me that these momentous changes occurred without any real upheaval. Except for the visit to the camp and the arrival of the six soldiers, I cannot think of any other memorable events. This may have been because our living conditions did not change immediately. How could they? I had to go back to the University and, for the moment, there was no possibility of moving out of the Ghetto or leaving China. Leaving China was all everyone talked about.

Where would we be going next?

I got my second malaria attack when I went back to the University in September. It was a very warm day and I started shivering. I tried to make it home by bicycle, but when I started throwing up, I had to load the bike and myself on a rickshaw. Thanks to Father's care, this was my last attack. He gave me enough medicine to turn me yellow all over, but it did the trick. Father had also recovered from another brush with death, his second in five years, and was thinking about how to re-establish his medical practice.

My big break came when the Shanghai American Private School reopened late in September or early October 1945. Not only did I get my job back, which was financially vital, but I also could move out of the Ghetto to a nice room on the school grounds.

The biggest difficulty was the scheduling conflict between my classes at the University and my teaching assignment. I simply could not attend morning classes at the University. I distinctly remember going to Father Andre Bonnichon, the dean of the law school to explain to him that I really had no choice. I had to teach to eat, since all my tutoring pupils were now back in school and I was not giving private lessons. He insisted that I had to attend all classes, but I sensed that he understood my predicament and I decided to take my chances to teach school in the morning, usually until one o'clock, and attend classes at the University in the afternoon. I remember being called in by the dean about missing too many classes. I made my excuses. A month later I was called into the office of the rector to be told that I must attend my classes. I explained why I could not and implied that the dean had given me permission to do what I did. This happened at least one more time during the second semester. I am quite certain that everyone knew my circumstance, but wanted to

Aurora University

help me, and continued the reprimands to keep up appearances. The fact that I took all the exams, excusing myself from teaching when necessary, and kept up very good grades eventually got me through.

I finished the fall semester first among the five foreign students taking the same program, none of whom had to hold down jobs. It was extremely difficult to juggle all this, but I suppose living again under normal conditions with enough money, even enough to help my parents, made it look easy compared to the previous two years. I am still proud of how I dealt with my final exams, particularly the oral examinations. When I could not arrange otherwise, I rode to the University between class periods, took the exam and went back to teaching. Unk Cheney also was very understanding. So, I managed to graduate in June of 1946 with a law degree, just one tenth of a point behind Joseph Takoah, who later emigrated to Israel and became its ambassador to the

Aurora Graduation Spring 1946-Paul(back row third from right)
(Joseph Takoah back row center)

United Nations.

My life as a school teacher was clearly at an end. Former teachers at the American School had returned to Shanghai. Once again, by a stroke of luck, one of the teachers was Tres Kops, whose husband, Paul, was the number two partner in the American law firm of Allman, Kops and Lee.

Tres suggested I go see Mr. Kops, and so began my career as a lawyer.

14

YOUNG SHANGHAI LAWYER

THE NEED FOR foreign lawyers in Shanghai goes back to the days when Shanghai was established as an International Settlement in 1863. There were no restrictions on foreign lawyers practicing in Shanghai. Since many foreign and American firms did business in China, (who could ignore a market of 400 million people?), there was a definite need for someone to advise these businessmen, who preferred their own nationals to Chinese advisors. Though many businesses had to suspend operations during World War II, as soon as the War was over, business streamed back into Shanghai and Allman, Kops, and Lee was reopened. It had been founded by Judge Norwood Allman, who was not only an important influence on my life, but one of the most interesting people I ever met.

Norwood F. Allman was born a Virginia farm boy in 1893. After college, he entered the diplomatic service. He was sent to Peking in 1915 as a Student Interpreter to the American legation and eventually became a consular official. According to his book *Shanghai Lawyer* he eventually became Vice Consul in a provincial capital. At that time, he married the daughter of American missionaries, Mary Louise Hamilton. The fact that Mrs. Allman had gone to Wellesley with Mei Lin Soong, later known as Madame Chiang Kai-shek, was an asset to the Allmans' social position, and the Judge's business, once Chiang became president of China. The Judge left the Foreign Service because he could not stand the formalities that were part and parcel of being a diplomat. He resented having to talk to people he did not want to talk to, having to dress formally and to attend dinners and other functions. He joined a law office in 1925 and was very successful, certainly being helped by his fluent knowledge of Chinese, but primarily because of his exceptional integrity and courage. The Chinese trusted him implicitly and deservedly.

The Judge was generous to a fault with his friends, an excellent horseman and a hard drinker, an important quality in foreign outposts. In the mid-1930s he became an assessor at the Shanghai Municipal Court, a court independent of Chinese jurisdiction, which dealt with legal problems of the foreign community and crimes committed by foreigners. The latter provision was of great importance to foreigners who did not want to be subjected to the very cruel regulations of Chinese criminal law. This is where Mr. Allman acquired the nickname "Judge", which stayed with him for the rest of his life. When the Japanese invaded China in the 1930s, the Judge knew exactly where he stood. He hated the Japanese with a passion, which put his safety at considerable risk. When the Chinese editor of the largest Chinese language paper in Shanghai, *Shun Pao*, fled because of threats to his life, the Judge became the newspaper's editor. The paper ardently supported the Chinese government and was bombed by the Japanese. The Judge received personal threats as well. He had to have a bodyguard at all times, even at the law office. When the War in the Pacific broke out in December 1941, the Judge was in Hong Kong. I was told he was there on business, but I have often wondered whether he was not warned to leave Shanghai. Apparently, the Japanese who captured him in Hong Kong did not recognize him and he was eventually repatriated to the United States after six months in the Stanley Internment Camp in some kind of an exchange agreement. Mrs. Allman and their youngest son, John, who were stuck in Shanghai, were also repatriated at the same time. On his return to the States, he was given an important job with the Far Eastern desk of the OSS, the forerunner of the CIA. One wonders if this association was the Allman's ticket home, while others had to spend the War in internment camps.

With the return of foreigners to China in 1945, reconstruction was necessary and everyone's hopes ran high. Of course, many came back for the easy life that Shanghai offered due to cheap labor, including household servants. A foreigner sent by his company to China was a privileged individual. Being paid in US dollars was the key, since the dollar was the almighty currency in those days. But there was more to this than money. There was the feeling of superiority possessed by foreigners that had been nurtured over the one hundred and twenty years since the Opium Wars. Political weakness and turmoil in China created a situation where the Chinese needed help and foreigners saw this as an opportunity. The Chinese people were poor and most had to work cheaply. While the superior attitude of the foreigners was obviously wrong and not justified, it was not easy to remain free of it. I am sure I was occasionally as guilty as others, but I always maintained a great respect for the innate intelligence and industriousness of the Chinese people.

Paul Kops was the number two partner in the firm, generally a very nice guy, much impressed with what he had achieved, but otherwise not particularly interesting. The third partner, Jim Davies, retired within a year after I joined Allman, Kops and Lee and was replaced by a Chinese associate, James Lee. James was educated in China, very bright, capable, and very rich, at least partially due to the fact that he had married into a wealthy family. James and I generally got along, but a little more about him later.

As it has happened in my career, the interview with Paul Kops was fairly short, and even before I had reached home, there was a message to come to work the following Monday. It was the end of June 1946. Shanghai in 1946 was quite an extraordinary place; maybe not more extraordinary than before, but in a different way. The change from wartime was dramatic. Foreigners and their money streamed in and everybody tried to grab a piece of the pie. Unfortunately, Chiang Kai-shek decided that the defeat of the Communists was more important than anything else. The United States tried to help Chiang with money and military advice, but could not control his actions and as we know today, he was unable to achieve his goals.

I will revisit the political situation in China several times. The next six years of my life was determined by what was happening in Chinese society. In retrospect, I lean towards the belief that even if Chiang had not made so many mistakes, and the corruption in the government had not been as terrible as it was, the Communists would have eventually won anyway. It seems that there was a certain inevitability in the rise of Communism in China as an aftermath of World War II, just as there had been in Europe after World War I.

While I was starting to build my career, the refugee community overwhelmingly opted to leave as quickly as possible to wherever they could. The Praegers, my sister Licci, Heinz and Jack, left for the United States on a US Navy transport ship in 1947. Heinz, having been born in Germany, was able to obtain a quota number earlier than those of us who had been born in Austria. The United States immigration law, The Johnson-Reed Act, was enacted in 1924 with the objective of keeping people considered less desirable out of the United States. Quota numbers were based on the population in the United States in 1890, before the great waves of immigrants from Italy, Ireland and Eastern Europe had arrived. The quota allowed for two percent of the population of a nationality each year. The law obviously favored the British, although there was hardly any immigration from England and Scotland. There was also a large German population in the States, the descendants of the Hessians who fought in the Revolutionary War. Thus, refugees born in Germany could get a quota number fairly easily, as long as an affidavit of support was provided by someone in the States. Uncle Richard provided the affidavit for the Praegers. The affidavit of support meant that the giver of the affidavit guaranteed that the new immigrants would not become a public charge. The situation was quite different from today when immigrants, legal or otherwise, are provided with all kinds of assistance from the government.

At this point in time I felt I really had no place to go. Returning to Vienna seemed out of the question, although some people did, my cousin Erwin being one. (Within a few years Erwin and family left Austria and came to the States.) Israel was not a realistic possibility until after its creation in May 1948, and by that time I was doing very well and was prepared to gamble on a future in China. In fact, the three years until the Communists marched into Shanghai in May 1949, were years of unbroken success and excitement. It is a little difficult to describe these three years without sounding boastful. When I got the job, I literally had to use the family's last twenty dollars to buy a suit. By the time the Communists occupied Shanghai three years later, I had set up my parents in a nice apartment in the French Concession and furnished the place so that Father could restart his practice. I had a car, a bank account in the States and was a member of the American Club. We had two servants and a chauffeur so that my parents could use the car while I was at work.

How did that all happen in such a short time to a very young man? Certainly, it was my good fortune to be at the right place at the right time. The firm needed me as much as I needed them. There were just not many people with my education available at that time in Shanghai. Bringing a young lawyer from the States would have involved several times the cost and considerable delay, thus the firm was more than willing to give me a chance. My record, both as a teacher and student, was excellent, my family background was satisfactory, and while I do not think that being Jewish played any part in the decision to hire me, it became an asset since the firm had many Jewish clients.

Hamilton House-September 2019

I started out as a combination bookkeeper and general factotum. I vividly remember the first day at 208 Hamilton House at the intersection of Foochow and Kiangsu Roads, opposite the Municipal Building. I reported to Paul Kops, who reached into his desk drawer and produced bundles of US dollars. My first job was to count the money and put it into a safe deposit box at the Chase Bank. There was about twenty thousand dollars, a small fortune at the time, the equivalent of at least a quarter million US dollars today. The firm certainly had confidence in me. I then set up a set of books and little by little was given some legal work. At first, it was mostly routine work in connection with meetings of the China Trade Act companies, but soon I did a substantial amount of legal work, including contracts and negotiations. I remained in charge of accounts, but hired a bookkeeper to do the routine tasks within the year.

I came to function as the office manager, except for the right to hire and fire staff. Since nearly all the staff were Chinese, relations with the Chinese employees were James Lee's responsibility. It was no wonder that my initial and quick success made me a bit overbearing, although I did not realize it at the time. Feelings of being displaced may have led to jealousy by one or two of the long-time Chinese employees. One evening, James Lee called me into his office and explained the enormous importance of maintaining face in Chinese society and that I was stepping on some toes. Then, at the end of our talk, in what I consider a very Chinese manner, he asked me what my salary was. He said that it wasn't enough and that he would see to it that I got a substantial increase. From then on, I heeded his advice and my relationship with Mr. Lee was very good, and remained so until his death in Taiwan in 1970. (In one of the ironies of life, by that time, I was in a position to send legal work to his law firm, Lee & Li in Taiwan.) But, the employees did not forget my *faux pas* and struck back when the Communists came to power. A situation which I will recount later on.

Shortly after I joined Allman, Kops and Lee, Aurora University asked whether I could teach the Finance Mathematics course. This was the course which originally had attracted me to the University, and in which I had excelled. The professor, a former Czech diplomat, wanted to return home. I had to ask permission from the Partners at the firm since I had to leave early once a week. They agreed to me accepting this assignment. Having someone teach at a university was good for the firm's image. (James Lee taught law at another university.)

Here I was, just twenty six years old, with a good job at an

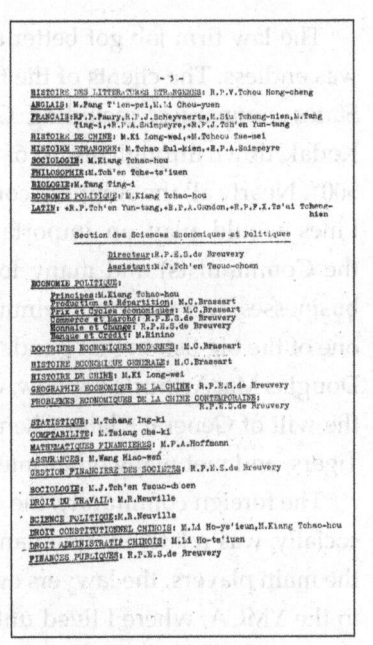

Directory of Faculty and Students – Aurora University 1948-1949

American law firm and teaching once a week at a French Jesuit university. All this happened just eight years after I had to leave Vienna as a refugee, with ten dollars in my pocket, having survived extremely difficult living conditions, including serious illness. To this day, I sometimes have difficulty grasping how I managed to accomplish this under such challenging circumstances. I think it was a combination of will power and the determination not to be poor. It was more than simple ambition. It was the desire and drive to live properly, to be someone. Money came with the effort put forth, but if money was the only driving force, I wouldn't have accepted the teaching position at Aurora University. The compensation was a pittance given the considerable amount of work required to prepare the lectures and exams in French. I taught until 1949 when the Communists purged all foreigners from the University.

The law firm job got better all the time. The variety of cases was endless. The clients of the firm included many large United States companies, including General Electric, Coca-Cola and Kodak, down through the list of what is today called the "Fortune 500". Nearly all the shipping companies, (of which United States Lines would play an important role during my time under the Communists) and many local Chinese and foreign-owned businesses, were clients. Swimming in a small pond, attached to one of the big fish in that pond, was to my benefit. I met General Douglas MacArthur's nephew, who wanted a divorce, witnessed the will of General Claire Chennault, commander of the Flying Tigers, and met many other interesting and well-known people.

The foreign community, the one that counted in business and socially, was relatively small and I was connected with some of the main players, the lawyers everyone consulted. I soon moved to the YMCA, where I lived until I rented an apartment in 1947 in the French Concession on Route Vallon. My parents were now able to move out of Hongkew, too, giving Father an opportunity to try to reestablish his practice.

Getting an apartment was no small undertaking due to the scarcity of available places. You had to pay key money to the landlord. The key money gave you the right to move in. You still had to pay rent. I think I paid $5,000.00 in key money, a lot of money at the time, about one and half years of income for me. I did not have that much money and had to borrow it from our friend, Bertha Ellig, who had inherited some money from her brother. Over the years, I had become her financial manager. I was able to repay her within three years, but could only recoup half of the key money I had paid. Once the Communists had gained control and my parents left Shanghai in August 1950, it was best to sell quickly and get what I could.

In 1947, I acquired an army surplus jeep. What an adventure

it was to ride in it, particularly when it rained! A little later I bought a car. I also became a member of the American Club. Both the car and the membership were acquired on the urging of the Partners. They believed I needed these amenities to properly represent them and raised my salary so that I could afford all this. The Judge lent me a pony, Felix, which I had to support. Rumor had it that it was easier to make a career in the firm if one could ride. Both the Judge and Paul Kops were avid horsemen and polo players.

Paul riding Felix

Riding was certainly a social asset, just like golf is today. So I tried to learn, and while I was never really good at it, I enjoyed going out on weekends to ride through the countryside. I would never have made the polo team. I tried playing polo once and knew I could never master the necessary skills. I did have various adventures with my horse, like when Chinese children threw firecrackers under Felix on Chinese New Year and I took a nice tumble. Or when the horse did not want to cross a small bridge and I had to lead it across. Felix was so happy to be on the other side that he accelerated and stepped on my foot. As throughout my life, my luck held. I never broke anything, just acquired some painful bruises.

I now started to travel a little bit into the interior of China. The first Christmas holiday while I was with the firm, I went to visit my cousin, Erwin, who had found a position as a doctor in a missionary hospital in Yu Yao, a port about one hundred miles south of Shanghai. When the English missionaries were interned by the Japanese, Erwin, his wife and their two children remained the only foreigners in this city of over 100,000 people. As a doctor he was very much needed and so they were able to survive the War without too much difficulty. I traveled both ways by train to Hangchow, but on the way to Yu Yao from Hangchow, Erwin had arranged for me to be picked up by an UNRRA, United Nations Relief and Rehabilitation Administration, truck that was bringing supplies in. What an experience to travel over these roads in an open truck! I got to Yu Yao so dusty I nearly looked like a clown in the circus. Everyone immediately knew where I was going. After all, there was only one foreign family in town. On the way back I took a bus, which went to the river at Hangchow. I may have been the first white man to ever ride on that bus. I had to take the ferry across the river and then a rickshaw to the railroad station. I still feel it was remarkable that I never felt unsafe, the only foreigner in a sea of Chinese faces. Maybe I was just naive, but I give credit to the Chinese people, who while showing a lot of curiosity, never made me feel threatened. My parents went to visit Erwin a few months later, but they were able to go by coastal steamer, a much easier way to travel.

Girlfriends continued to play an important role in my life. Once, someone in the office very discreetly hinted that involvement with the wrong person could be harmful to one's career. The warning referred to my obvious interest in my Russian secretary. We did go out, but it probably was fortunate she did not reciprocate the attention and I moved on. At Easter, I took a weekend trip to Hangchow with a girlfriend. Hangchow is a beautiful spot on a lake which has many little islands with pavilions on them. Hills surround the lake; it all looks like a Chinese painting.

PAUL HOFFMANN

My first plane trip took me to visit my good friend Victor Donath in Nanking, where he worked for the United States Army. I think the Army kept a presence in China in an advisory capacity until late in 1948. Victor came to the States and eventually settled near Los Angeles, California. We remained lifelong friends.

My final trip outside Shanghai was my summer vacation in August 1948 to Moganshan, a resort about 250 miles from Shanghai. It is atop a mountain, which could only be reached by walking up or being carried up in a sedan chair. I drove there as a passenger with a friend whose family spent the summer there to escape the dreadful Shanghai heat and humidity. Our route was through Hangchow. The condition of the roads was such that one had to carry two spare tires. We needed them both before we came to the first garage. We were also held up by a thunderstorm. Then the Chinese army blocked the road with its trucks while the soldiers ate their dinner. They would not budge. I could not persuade my friend to spend the night in Hangchow. We drove on and soon found out we had picked the wrong turn at a crossroads. At about ten o'clock at night we came to the end of the road and a Chinese lumber camp. The Chinese there were quite surprised to have these two foreigners, neither of whom spoke Chinese, drop in on them in the middle of the night. We quickly understood that we had to go back to the intersection.

One has to picture the situation. There was no one on the road but us. Had we run out of gas or had another flat, we would certainly have had a long wait for help. We finally arrived at one o'clock in the morning at the foot of the mountain and I took a sedan chair to the top. My macho friend insisted on walking. The next morning someone approached me to ask whether I had heard about the two crazy guys who had come up the mountain well after midnight.

Moganshan is a beautiful place, so beautiful and relatively cool that Chiang Kai-shek also came there for his summer holidays. I actually saw him as he was carried past my hotel in a sedan chair, less than ten feet away. Looking back, it is remarkable that there did not appear to be any security, no roads were closed, and there were no armed soldiers; all this in the middle of a ferocious civil war. China did have its share of assassinations and kidnappings, and Chiang certainly could have been a target since he was despised by many. One has to wonder what has happened to make today's extreme security measures for heads of state, or other important people, so necessary.

I spent a week in Moganshan, unfortunately, suffering from one of the very bad colds with which I have often been plagued. At the end of the week, I took a safer route by bus and train to return to Shanghai. There would be no trips outside of Shanghai for the next three and half years.

15

THE COMMUNIST STORM STRIKES:
AUGUST 1948 – AUGUST 1949

I PARTICULARLY remember my stay in Moganshan because it coincided with the revaluation of the Chinese currency which was accomplished by dividing the exchange rate by a factor of four million. This was a last ditch effort to stem the unbelievable rate of inflation. It had climbed to 12 million Chinese Yuan: 1 US dollar. The plan was to eventually return to the three to one exchange rate that was in effect at the time of the Japanese invasion in 1937. Due to the pressures of the war with the Japanese, the Chinese currency continued to weaken steadily, as more and more money was printed to support the conflict.

At the end of World War II, money was needed for reconstruction. The rate of inflation accelerated to a point only exceeded in Germany after the First World War. One contributing factor was the incredible corruption at all levels of the Chinese government. While no one ever openly accused Chiang, his brothers-in-law, the Kungs, were among the worst offenders. Then there was the Chinese practice of paying a general the salary for all the troops he claimed were under his command, rather than paying individual soldiers directly. Most of the generals would overstate how many soldiers they commanded. In addition, when the generals got the money, they used it to buy gold or US dollars on the black market, thereby driving up the exchange rate. A month or so later, they sold the US dollars and gold at the higher price and paid the soldiers in Chinese Yuan, pocketing the difference. The generals got very rich and the purchasing power of the soldiers decreased each month. The Nationalist soldiers were reported to have exchanged their arms for food with the Communists, who were steadily advancing towards Shanghai. After the Communists took over Shanghai, I saw the Communist soldiers carrying US arms. Were they captured or bought? Who knows? Probably both scenarios had occurred. No wonder the soldiers were unwilling to put forth a good fight for the Nationalist cause.

If one was paid in US dollars, or had access to the black market, you could make a profit. I was paid in US dollars and sold dollars only when I needed extra cash. I had overdraft privileges at Chase Bank and was able to write checks in Yuan to get cash, large bundles in denominations as high as one hundred thousand Yuan. When the bank called to cover the overdraft every two weeks or so, the dollar had risen substantially against the Yuan, and I was able to exchange enough dollars on the black market to cover my overdraft. If I remember correctly, the overdraft privilege was not less than one hundred million Yuan. By this method, I was able to reduce my expenses in US dollars substantially. The office, which collected most of its fees in US dollars, operated in the same way, only on a larger scale. I was in charge of dealing with the black market broker. I have never quite understood how the banks made money under this system, but somehow they must have come up with a strategy. After all, the bank was not required to grant overdrafts.

There had to be losers in this scenario and it was the general population who could not protect itself from the rapid devaluation of the Yuan. Savings accounts based on Yuan were wiped out. People receiving salaries in Yuan could not buy enough food for the month. At Allman, Kops and Lee, we pegged the salaries of the Chinese employees to the US dollar. I was instrumental in advocating for this arrangement; a fact the staff did not seem to remember when there was terrible dissension in the office after the Communist takeover. At home, I would ask the servants every week whether

Paul's parents and the car April 1948

they had any money left and would give them more if they needed it. A fixed salary really had no meaning. At that time, we had a cook, a cleaning woman and a chauffeur. (I had hired the chauffeur predominantly so that my parents could use the car when I was at work, but it also was not wise for a foreigner to be his own driver. The smallest accident could escalate into a major incident. Sometimes an accident would be manufactured, such as a mother putting a child in front of the car and pulling it away, just as you were about to pull out. A hue and cry would ensue, a crowd would gather and the best one could do was to give the irate mother money to placate her.)

The reforms of August 1948 re-valued the Yuan and put severe penalties, including the death penalty, on black market dealings. Two or three prominent Chinese businessmen were executed early on, in an effort to end the unlawful practices, with no effect. The Chinese currency continued to plunge. By the time the Communists marched into Shanghai in late May 1949, the

Yuan had gone from 3:1 US dollars in 1937 to 20,000,000:1, a drop of 66,000%, over a period of ten months. Was it incredible that nothing was able to slow the rate of inflation? Yes, it was totally incomprehensible considering what was at stake.

Sometime in 1949, the accountant for the Flying Tigers, General Chennault's outfit, called me to pay their annual retainer, which had been set at $10,000.00 US, easily the equivalent of half a million dollars today. I asked him whether they would pay in US dollars or Chinese Yuan. When the accountant said they planned to pay in Yuan, I told him I had to find out what the conversion rate would be that day. I called the black market broker for the current rate and I was told that a certain rate was effective until 11 AM. The broker was in my office at exactly 11 AM to pick up the check. That's how quickly the value of money was changing. Sometimes one bought gold, which was circulating in one and ten ounce bars, instead of US dollars. It is not surprising that this madness led to all kinds of fraud. US dollars were being counterfeited. There were bundles of Chinese currency with Yuan notes on the outside and newspapers on the inside. Who had the time to count that amount of money? The bundles got so large that I had to ask the office boy or chauffeur for help to carry them to the car.

A room could probably be filled with the books that have been written to explain the reasons for the Communist success in China. In my opinion, at that moment in history, the Communists had an idea to sell. The premise espoused by the Communists was that every societal problem was the fault of the rich, who had exploited the great masses of very poor peasants and workers. As described, the economic situation was desperate after ten years of war. There always had been an enormous gap between rich and poor in China; there was no real middle class. After the War, political corruption, always endemic in China, became simply awful and resulted in a total loss of confidence in the government. I also don't think that any realistic plan on how to better the lot of the Chinese people was ever put forth by the Nationalist Government.

The Communists had a monolithic dictatorial leadership, armed by the Russians, who had been trying to engineer a Communist takeover in China since the early 1920s. The starving peasants were promised that once they had won, they would own the land. It is of no use to discuss the value of these promises and their result. As I write this, history has spoken and shown that Communism as practiced in the 20th century did not work. However, it is easy to see how attractive this ideology was under the extreme circumstances prevailing at the time. Why did the Nationalists not treat their soldiers properly so that they would put up a good fight? I just don't know. Could it have been arrogance on the part of the Nationalist Party? Did they feel that they could not lose after defeating the Japanese and receiving support from the United States? Maybe history was just ripe for this change.

By April 1948, Shanghai was surrounded by the Communist forces. Only air and sea routes were open. James Lee left for Hong Kong. He was justifiably afraid of what could happen to him under the Communists. He was rich and was closely associated with Americans. Paul Kops decided that he wanted to take his home leave. I remember telling him to let Mr. Allman go instead, since the Judge was in much greater personal danger because of his very close connections to the Chiang government. Paul flatly refused and it remained for me to eventually make it possible for the Judge to leave, by acting as his proxy, saving him from certain arrest and a long imprisonment. This is not just speculation on my part. It happened to another prominent American lawyer, Cornell Franklin, who stayed behind and spent approximately eight months in the Haiphong Road Internment camp before leaving Shanghai in 1951.

A day or two before the Communists marched into Shanghai, I visited some friends who lived on the far outskirts, probably a mile or two from the frontline. They told me that we would hear the fighting at five o'clock because every day, exactly at 5 PM, the Nationalists started firing at the Communists. As predicted, exactly at 5 PM, there was some cannon fire. I decided there was no need to find out whether the Communists would fire back by going out to see what was happening; they could overshoot their target. That night, I was awakened by shots outside our windows. I looked out, being careful to keep my head below the windowsill, and saw some soldiers running and firing. A bullet lodged in the headboard of one of my friends' beds, waking them up rather rudely. The next morning, the Communists were in control of the city and for all intents and purposes, the civil war was over. The Communists had won. Eleven years and two months after Hitler's takeover of Austria had signaled the end of our life in Vienna, the end of our life in Shanghai had arrived. It did not come as a surprise, given all this stress, that Father would suffer his first heart attack just two weeks later.

As 1949 began, and it had become increasingly clear that the Communists would win the civil war and defeat the Nationalist government, most, but not yet all, of the Central European refugees had left. Other foreigners were advised to leave and many did. Among the White Russians, some were misled by the Soviet victories and offers of Soviet passports to go back to Russia. How many would regret this decision when they encountered the poor living conditions and lack of freedom in the Soviet Union? Russian Jews, except for the few who went back to Russia, migrated to wherever they could obtain a visa. Many went to Israel after the establishment of the State in May of 1948. There were those of us who hoped that the Communists would be more Chinese than Communist and not establish a Communist society. As had happened in previous crises in China, we thought it would be possible to find some kind of accommodation that would attempt to meet everyone's needs. Conditions had deteriorated so badly that everyone thought it just could not get any worse. But they did, just as conditions had worsened in Germany and Italy under their dictatorships. Human nature generally is not blessed with a great deal of foresight.

The question arises as to why I chose not to go to Israel. At the beginning of 1949, life was very difficult in Israel and I did not see how I would fit into Israeli society and earn a living given my education. I never was the pioneer type who could survive doing physical labor. Moreover, I had just invested in the apartment, had no extra money to spend and had incurred some additional debt. Lastly, life was good for me personally, and like everyone else who had not yet left, I hoped against hope that things would get better. However, I was sufficiently pessimistic about economic conditions and sold what little investments I had made in Shanghai companies. I suggested to my bosses that they do the same. They had difficulty imagining that everything would be lost. In fact that is what happened.

The changes came fairly rapidly. The United States did not recognize the Communist government and instituted an embargo. This action, plus its long-term support for Chiang, made the United States China's number one enemy. All businesses, and particularly foreign businesses, were considered the enemy of the people. There was no worse designation than "enemy of the people".[6]

Yet, in spite of the turbulent events, there was still time for

---

6   A good deal of what happened during the thirty three months I lived under the Communists is described in an article which I wrote for the Voice of America in 1952. This article together with some letters written during this period to my parents and Judge Allman are included in the appendix and in effect constitute a contemporaneous account of what happened once the Communists came to power. It is the closest I can come to a diary of these tumultuous times.

girls. There was Mary and Sophie and Mrs. Levine, but maybe the most important change in my life came early in September of 1949. I met Shirley.

16

SHIRLEY

I WENT TO a swim meet on September 3, 1949, the Saturday before Labor Day, at the Shanghai YMCA. I cannot imagine my life had I not gone. It is beyond comprehension how the course of one's life is changed by what on the surface appears to be an insignificant set of circumstances. I had gone to the swim meet with Sophie, a girl who I had been dating for about a year. I had become tired of chasing around; I was considering getting married. Sophie, who was barely 21 years old, just could not make up her mind. By the time we went to the swim meet, I had become less enthusiastic about Sophie.

Suddenly, there was this very attractive girl sitting next to me and I immediately liked what I saw. Sophie and Shirley didn't engage in conversation like two people who knew each other, but I found out later that Shirley not only knew Sophie and her family, but knew of me as well. Had they talked to each other, I certainly would have asked who Shirley was. I just remember thinking that Shirley must be Russian. I know we exchanged a few words because we shared a towel to shield us from the splashing swimmers. Three days later, on Tuesday, I was playing tennis with Sophie and there was Shirley watching us. Was she sending a message? We have debated this over the years. I think she was, but Shirley says it was a coincidence. (This is one argument that I am happy to let her win.) Then I took the initiative, and while Sophie changed out of her tennis outfit, I started talking to Shirley.

Given the times, it was easy to start a conversation by asking which country you intended to migrate to, since all foreigners knew they had to leave China sooner rather than later. I was surprised to find out Shirley planned to go to Israel. Just to keep the conversation going, I guessed that we were neighbors, and I was right. We lived less than two blocks from each other. I got her phone number, and wasting no time, called the next evening. It took a little persuasion. Shirley told me she was not going to play second fiddle to anyone. Those were her very words, but we went out a day or two later.

For Shirley and me, it was love at first sight. By late December we decided to get married. The engagement party was on January 8, 1950 and the wedding was held at the Ohel Moshe Synagogue on Ward Road in Hongkew on March 5, 1950. Shirley was three

Shirley and Paul Leaving the Ohel Moshe Synagogue – March 5, 1950

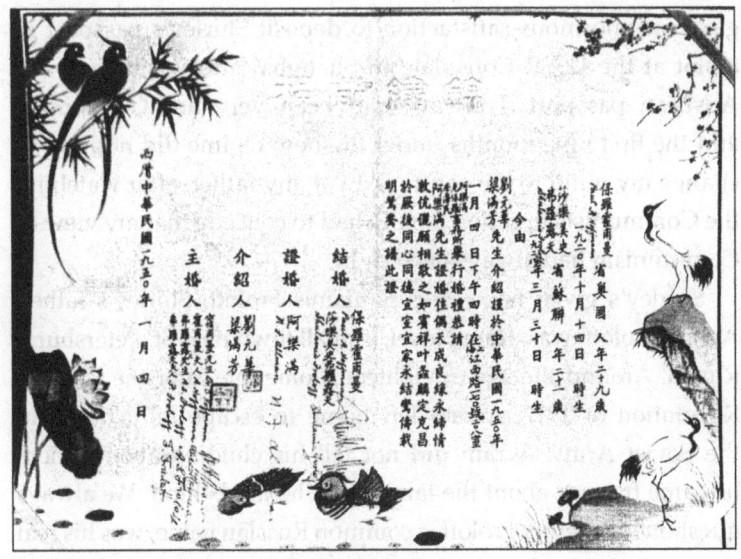

Chinese Wedding Certificate

weeks shy of her 22nd birthday and I was 29 years old.[7]

We took steps to marry legally on January 6, 1950 in the office of Allman, Kops and Lee. Witnesses signed our Chinese wedding document, acknowledging that we had agreed to marry, which was all that was required under Chinese law.

We did not consider this our real wedding, but the Austrian Embassy was about to close and I needed documentation that we were married to get an Austrian passport for Shirley. For all intents and purposes, Shirley was stateless. She had a Soviet passport, which her father had obtained for her in 1945 when she was seventeen years old, not yet of age. Having a Soviet passport was slightly better than not having any at all, as long as one did not make the mistake of going to Russia. The Soviet passport really was only a one-way ticket back to Russia. It

---

[7] See Appendix: Wedding Story: This Is The Story Of How Paul and Shirley Got Married – Humorous Recount of the Wedding Day, March 5, 1950. Sent to family and friends who had already left Shanghai.

gave me enormous satisfaction to deposit Shirley's passport in a slot at the USSR Consulate in Shanghai after I obtained her Austrian passport. I always had been very anti-Communist and the first nine months under the new regime did nothing to change my mind to the contrary. Even my father, after watching the Communists in action, finally had to concede that my view of Communism had always been right.

Shirley's given name was Shulamis Froloff. Shirley's father, Avram Froloff, was from Nevel, a small town near St. Petersburg, Russia. Around the age of eighteen, sometime after the Russian Revolution of 1917, Avram left home to escape induction into the Soviet Army. Avram did not tell his children about where he came from or about the family that he left behind. We always questioned whether Froloff, a common Russian name, was his real name, or whether he adopted it to shield his family from possible reprisals. The story he told was that he hitchhiked for a whole year from St. Petersburg across Siberia to Harbin, Manchuria.[8] A look at the map is enough to convince one of the difficulties he must have experienced. Besides the weather, there was fighting between the Red and White Russians. Unfortunately, I never had an opportunity to talk to him about his adventures. Avram was not the talkative type, and he was not skilled enough in English for long conversations, but he was a very nice man. I had less than a year from the time I met Avram until he and my mother-in-law, Fanya, left Shanghai for Israel to join their son, Tuvia, who was serving in the Israeli Defense Force. Regrettably, I really never got

---

8   Editor's Note: In 2016, 3 ½ years after Shirley's death. I was contacted by George Frolov, Shirley's first cousin, who informed me that Avram left his parents and seven brothers and sisters in Nevel. His whereabouts remained a mystery to the family he left behind. The Frolovs had all become devout Soviets, served in the military, and remained in the area around St. Petersburg. George and his family came to the United States in 1979. He found Shirley's obituary through an internet search. Unbeknownst to both of them, they had been living in Connecticut, just 5 miles apart, for the last ten years of Shirley's life.

to know him well. He died at age fifty-two in Israel from stomach cancer in November 1951.

Shirley's mother was born Fanya Egudkin in 1903 in Novozybkov, a town northwest of Gomel, Russia. Fanya's family left Russia to escape a very difficult life and the Communists some time before 1920. They went to Harbin, where there was a large White Russian community, including relatives who had immigrated there a few years earlier. Shirley's grandfather, Tuvia Egudkin, died of dysentery shortly after arriving in Harbin, leaving her grandmother, Golda Riva, to bring up their three youngest girls. Golda had twelve pregnancies, six boys and six girls. Five of the boys had died young and the sixth son drowned in the river as a young man. Golda's three eldest daughters were already married and remained in Gomel when Tuvia and Golda decided to move to Harbin. What a struggle it must have been for Golda to raise her three young daughters! But there was a network of caring relatives in Harbin to help out.

Shirley's parents were married in 1924 in Harbin. Their first child, a girl, Manya, was born in 1924, but died at the age of nine of typhoid fever. Shirley was born in 1928 and Tuvia, whom everyone called Teva, was born in 1931. Shirley began Russian school in 1935 at the age of seven. Manchuria had become a Japanese puppet state and as the war with China heated up, life became more difficult, and I imagine more unpleasant for foreigners. Shirley tells of famines; times when she had to stand in line for bread.

It is clear from what Shirley recounted that her family struggled. Her father did not have a profession. He worked as a sewing machine mechanic and tried all kinds of jobs, often working for relatives, but it was difficult to make ends meet most of the time. Shirley's mother assisted where she could. For example, Fanya helped with the baking of matzah for Passover in

Shirley and Teva – Summer in Harbin circa 1938

order to obtain the family's share for free. And Grandmother was there to help watch the children. Shirley often spoke about her grandmother, always with great love and respect. She preferred to remember the good times in Harbin, especially the dacha, the little summer cottage across the Sungari River, where she would spend the summer gardening with her Grandmother Golda.

Like many other Russians, the Froloffs moved to Shanghai in 1940, again preceded by relatives, specifically the Singaus family. Fanya's older sister, Genia, had married Mr. Singaus who did very well after moving to Shanghai and opened the Kamchatka Fur store on Bubbling Well Road.

In Shanghai, Shirley went to the Shanghai Jewish School, but in 1944, when she was just sixteen years old, left school to go to work as a secretary to help the family. Shirley's father again worked at a variety of jobs, including smuggling ball bearings and mercury through the Japanese lines from the North in a bicycle tire inner tube around his waist to avoid the border guards.

Shirley's mother was able to help out in Shanghai by taking in lunch guests. We all lived a very precarious existence in those days, and Shirley and I had the shared experience of going to work very early in our lives to help support our families.

Looking back over the years, I still marvel at the confluence of events that brought us together. We would have not found each other if it hadn't been for the political upheavals in the world. First the Russian Revolution of 1917 brought Shirley's family to Harbin. Then the advent of the Nazis, forced me to flee to Shanghai. And finally, the Sino-Japanese War in China brought Shirley's family, the Froloffs, to Shanghai.

Even though we started our married life under extremely difficult circumstances, we did not pay much attention to what was happening outside of our little world, at least for the first few months. It was impossible for a foreigner to travel anywhere, so we spent our honeymoon in a suite on the tenth floor of the Park Hotel, opposite the Race Course. There were several days when we had to walk up the ten flights of stairs because of an attack on the power company by the Nationalist Air Force (then based in Taiwan), which resulted in power shortages. Our first apartment was very comfortable; it had belonged to a client who had left Shanghai. I continued to go to the office every day, although there was not too much to do, and Shirley continued with her job at the Shanghai Gas Company. For lunch, we usually met at Shirley's parents' house where her mother prepared our meal. I was still a member of the French Club, where I unsuccessfully tried to teach Shirley to swim and play tennis. There were still dances and I have fond memories of the Bastille Day Party on July 14, 1950. We knew very well that the end of the good life, or what was left of it, was near. Plans to leave were the main topic of conversation among foreigners, just as it had been twelve years earlier in Vienna among Jews. Refugee transports were being

```
   38 ☼              Deutsche Post         Telegramm
              aus  SHANGHAI  CD 505 15  18 1606
   Aufgenommen      FUNK  PEKING BERLIN              Befördert
Tag  Monat Jahr Zeit                         Tag      Zeit
 18.10.50 1730       -LT-HOFFMANN LAGER      an      durch
 BRUECK. durch RUE.    WILDFLECKEN BL A6
 Amt


   ALL HEALTHY HOPE DEPARTURE  MARCH WRITTING WEEKLY
   = LOVE SHIRLEY  PAUL =
```

Telegram to Paul's parents in Germany

organized and both my parents and Shirley's parents decided to leave.

My parents left on a refugee transport in September of 1950. The destination was Wildflecken Displaced Persons Camp in northern Bavaria.[9] They went from Shanghai to Tientsin by train and then boarded a ship that traveled to Japan, Hawaii, through the Panama Canal to Italy, finally arriving in Germany after two months. They were there for another eight months before they were able to come to the United States.

The Froloffs went to Israel early in 1951 to join Teva, who had left Shanghai in 1949. I believe they extended their visas in order to stay in Shanghai a little longer in order to attend our wedding.

I made the decision to stay in Shanghai and see what

---

9   Editor's note: Paul wrote to his sister, who was already in the United States, "...parents happily departed on Wednesday, September 6 (1950) at 7:15...We brought them to the train at 1 o'clock...Since it was a mass transport, we were not allowed to go on the platform..."

happened. The decision was made easier by the fact that we both still had jobs and were likely to keep them for a while. I just could not bear the thought of being a penniless refugee again, and leaving on a refugee boat meant just that. The stories my parents told me about their trip and their stay in the Displaced Persons Camp in Germany before arriving in the United States confirmed that my fears were justified.

I now know that I risked my life by staying in Shanghai. But, at the time I did not think it wise to start a marriage on a refugee boat with all its stresses, not to speak of the unavoidable proximity to parents and relatives. The ensuing year and a half in China and the subsequent fourteen months of travel, were certainly difficult and stressful for a young marriage. However, I believe these first three years laid a foundation of trust. The knowledge of having shared and overcome great obstacles served us well for the rest of our lives.

17

LIFE UNDER THE COMMUNISTS:
AUGUST 1950 – FEBRUARY 1952

BY AUGUST 1950, five months after our wedding, it became increasingly clear that all foreigners, but primarily Americans, were in great personal danger. Judge Allman was high on the list, presumably because of his close connections with Chiang Kai-shek and the many other prominent Chinese people he connected with during his long stay in China. Foreigners could not get an exit visa unless they had discharged all their obligations to their Chinese employees. The firm had taken over the management of a number of its clients to permit their American managers to leave. The most important client was United States Lines, which still had about fifty employees. For the Judge to get an exit visa he needed someone to take over as his representative, and for the reasons explained at the end of the last chapter, I agreed.

The deal I made with the Judge was that I would stay in Shanghai and complete all the necessary transactions to shut down the firm. United States Lines, had negotiated an agreement with its employees before its American manager had left. I was to receive US$5,000 per month from US Lines to pay the expenses of their office. Whatever other funds I needed to keep the office and the Judge's household going were to come from the United States or fees paid to the firm in Shanghai. My salary was to be

Allman's house-Shirley and her parents Shirley with servant & dogs

continued, until I reached the United States. My salary was $400 per month, a substantial sum in those days since it was not taxed and the dollar's purchasing power was high. I also negotiated first class passage to America for Shirley and I and severance pay that was the equivalent of several months' salary. We also moved into the Judge's house at 179 Fah Hwa Road on the outskirts of town.

Judge Allman left early in October 1950, and at the age of thirty I found myself in charge of a law firm, a branch of a major shipping company, various other smaller businesses and the Allman household, including their five servants. At least seventy people looked to me for their paychecks. Judge Allman would later say that I saved his life, as well as the lives of those who were able to leave because the firm had taken over their responsibilities. He wrote this in a letter to the State Department in an effort to expedite our visas. Did he exaggerate? Maybe, in an effort to bring home the seriousness of the situation. I know of no American civilian who died in a Communist prison, but many were arrested. Prominent American lawyers in Shanghai, like Cornell Franklin, were arrested and spent more than a year in prison. I am fairly certain allowing Judge Allman to leave when he did, spared him imprisonment. There is no question that the Judge was lucky to get out substantially unharmed.[10]

Was it worth it for me to remain in Shanghai for as long as I did? That's hard to say. Would arriving two years earlier in the United States, albeit penniless, have had a favorable impact on my career? I do not think so. Did my experiences with the Communists impact the course of my life? Again, I do not think so. The one intrinsic value of this experience was the feeling of having overcome great difficulties, which helped my self-confidence later in life. However, after all was said and done, we had a pleasant trip to Europe and a fairly good stay in Vienna and Italy while we were waiting for our United States visas, without worries about money. Obviously, there is nothing that is worth risking your life for, but in retrospect, I believe that the good and the bad probably balanced out.

Shortly after I took over the operation of Allman, Kops and Lee something unexpected happened. I had some pain in my right groin which was diagnosed as a chronic inflammation of the appendix and I was advised to have it taken out. If the inflammation flared up into appendicitis it would be very serious. My thought process was that in the near future I could be traveling where medical help may not be readily available, such as on the train trip from Shanghai to Hong Kong, or on the ocean voyage to Europe. I therefore decided to proceed with the operation, since taking out an appendix was not considered a difficult operation in Shanghai in 1950. Nonetheless, the operation nearly killed me, and the lesson learned is never to go under the knife unless really necessary. The doctors claimed the appendix was in fact inflamed, but I still have my doubts. What

---

10 See Appendix: Communications Between Paul, Judge Allman, United States Lines, Staff of Allman, Kops and Lee, Secretary of the Treasury, Federal Reserve Bank and Congressional Representative Francis E. Walter regarding settlement of affairs in Shanghai: Staff Severance Letter, PAH to NFA 2-12-51 NFA to Sec. of Treasury 2-17-51, NFA to Federal Reserve Bank 3-16-51, NFA to US Lines 3-17-51, NFA to Rep. Walter 4-21-51

else were they going to say? Three days after the operation, an embolism developed and traveled to my lung, a very serious and dangerous complication with a very low survival rate. The doctors had in fact given up on me. What probably saved my life was a new blood thinner, Heparin, that had just come on the market. Shirley went from pharmacy to pharmacy and literally bought up all that was available. I remember that I knew I was dying and I thought that this was really unfair since we had been married only seven months. I was also worried that Shirley might be pregnant and what would happen to her since we hardly had any money at that time. My one consolation was that the employees depending on me, or rather holding me hostage for what they thought was due to them, would no longer have anyone to torture. I was not far off the mark in my thinking, because when the employees heard how sick I was, they were not ashamed to approach Shirley, asking her to send a telegram to Mr. Allman to appoint someone else as his proxy in case I died. They did not care about the feelings of this young bride in grave danger of losing her husband. To her great credit, Shirley refused and did not tell me about this episode until I was well recovered. I fooled everyone and survived the critical night. The crisis ended when I coughed up a blood clot as large as a small fist. I can still hear myself saying "I nearly died now." The doctor confirmed that I was right. Is dying difficult? It did not seem so. Maybe I was too drugged, or too weak to know better, but it just felt like I was floating. After that night, the fever broke and I slowly started to recover.

Before I was ready to go back to work, in late November 1950, the Chinese had entered the war in Korea. Once again, external influences had created havoc in my life. As a result of the Chinese intervention, the United States froze all Chinese funds in the United States, which in effect meant that no money could be sent to China without permission from the Treasury Department. So here I was responsible for the salaries of seventy people and had no money.

Because China was now a dictatorship, the truth about what was happening in Korea was easily perverted. When the Korean War started in June 1950, it was clear to everyone that the North had invaded the South. The only remaining English newspaper in Shanghai printed the true story, including the rout of the Southern army. The next day, the paper was forced to print an apology to the effect that it was mistaken. The story now read that the South had attacked the North and the victorious People's Army was defeating the "running dogs" of the Imperialists. This was just like the lie Hitler had told the Germans; that Poland had attacked Germany. If the lie is large enough, it becomes plausible and everyone believes it. A Chinese friend who attended Aurora University with me, and who I got a job in the office, totally accepted this myth. I could not shake his belief that the South had attacked the North, even though all the facts showed that the South was totally unprepared for war.

United Nations troops were able to hold on to a corner of Korea. The landing at Inchon behind the North Korean lines turned the tide and the North Koreans suffered a devastating defeat. Through diplomatic channels, the Chinese warned that if the United Nations troops crossed the 38th parallel they would intervene. These warnings went unheeded. As I mentioned before, as Chinese troops marched in greater than usual numbers through Shanghai it was common knowledge that they were going to Korea. It was after I had left China that I read that General McArthur had testified before Congress that he did not know that the Chinese would intervene. This speaks very poorly for US Intelligence or McArthur's veracity. How could anyone believe that the Chinese Communists, riding high after their victory just one year earlier, could tolerate US troops on their borders and the ignominious defeat of a satellite state?

For me, the question was how to extricate myself from the very precarious position in which I now found myself. I remember making phone calls to the United States while still confined to bed. The calls were transmitted by radio and were plagued by interference. In addition, you had to be very careful what you said since the two countries were de facto at war, despite the fiction that the Korean War was a UN Police Action. I was told that the necessary steps to obtain a license for the release of funds from the US Department of the Treasury had been initiated. In retrospect, it took only seven months, but that was a very long time to be besieged by very unhappy people who wanted their money and whose minds were poisoned daily by hostile propaganda.[11]

In the meantime I had to scrounge to make ends meet, not only for the office but also at home. Fortunately, Shirley kept on working at the Shanghai Gas Company so we had some money for our living expenses. I also was able to borrow money on the oral promise to repay once I was outside China. People were so desperate to get money out of China that they were satisfied with a promise. I remember repaying a thousand dollars, a generous sum in those days, to someone in Singapore when our boat stopped there in March 1952. As always, there were crooks who took advantage of the situation and there were some loans that were never repaid.

Naturally we had to curtail our standard of living. First, I sold the car. Everything I did required the permission of the Communist authorities. Soon thereafter, I paid off the five

---

11   See Appendix: Treasury Department License

servants I had inherited from Mr. Allman. I was able to sell the substantial amount of liquor Mr. Allman had in the house on the black market. I was lucky the servants did not denounce me. I suppose they were afraid that if they reported me they would not get their money. The Allman house was considered a United States property and was confiscated. We moved into two rooms with friends of Shirley, very much nearer to town.

I went to the office or to court every day and every day was difficult. There was one bright light in the office, our office boy, Peter Chang. He was the only one who never participated in the continuous harassment I experienced from the other staff. His English was very good and he was of enormous help to me until the day we left. What his motives were, I just do not know, but I never detected anything that would throw suspicion on his sincerity. Just like under the Nazis, you never knew when and where you would find a decent human being. I wish I could have kept in touch with Peter, but once we left it was not possible, and could even have been harmful to him. I do not know what became of him. Peter went everywhere with me; to court, to the police station, to the Labor Bureau. Although I did not understand what he translated, from his demeanor it appeared that he presented my side forcefully. Why the Communists let him get away with this and did not accuse him of being a "running dog of the capitalists", was, and still is, a mystery.

I was able to save a good deal of my correspondence from this time period. These communications document that I was able to run the office and provide services to clients. The days when either my staff or the US Lines staff held me captive in the office for hours were the worst. I could not even go to the bathroom or use the phone until they had achieved what they wanted, namely make me send another telegram to the United

States demanding money. I simply was not able to get across that I was as anxious as they were to get the situation resolved. They would not believe that I did not have the money to pay them out of my funds, or that I could not borrow the money. Of course, they were wrong.

Our life outside the office consisted of getting together with a few friends and a lot of card playing, either at home or at a friend's house. The conversation always revolved around the latest problems and how one could extricate oneself from them. The situation was nearly as bad as in Vienna in 1938 and during the last years of the War in 1944 and 1945.

Finally, in June of 1951, the money came to pay off my biggest problem, the fifty some employees at US Lines. It took eight months for the money to arrive in Shanghai. To me, it seemed like eight years. The Department of the Treasury insisted that the Communists arrange for me to leave in return for the $100,000 I was required to pay the staff and to settle two lawsuits for diverted cargo. The Chinese were not willing to guarantee anything and I was caught between two overwhelming adversaries. Eventually, the Treasury Department relented and accepted that I had applied for an exit visa as sufficient documentation.

It had been my policy not to go to the US Lines office because of the perceived danger of violence from the staff. But now that the news was good and all problems seemed resolved, I thought it was safe to go to the office to discuss the method of payment. I'll never forget that day, even though time seems to dim the worst memories. Those harrowing six hours were reminiscent of my experience on Jewish Boycott Saturday in Vienna in 1938. Looking back upon this experience, and the equally traumatic incident of holding the sign for the Nazis in front of the coffee house fourteen years earlier, it is interesting that my physical reaction was the same. While being held and threatened, I maintained calm, but as soon as I was released, I collapsed. In Shanghai, as soon as I got out into the fresh air and into a rickshaw I threw up. When we reached home, Shirley called the doctor because I was not feeling well and my heart was racing. It all was a reaction to the extreme stress and I had recovered by the next morning.

With the resolution of the US Lines problems I thought we would soon be able to leave, but it took another eight months. I had to close the law office and pay severance pay to the staff. All kinds of real or invented problems of former clients were laid at my door. The Chinese were always looking for the "responsible" person they could hold as a hostage. Other foreigners, who had been clients and were in trouble with their employees, or the authorities, would try to unload their problems on me. Some of these claims were bizarre to say the least.

I was fortunate that Mr. Hajek, a gentleman whom we had become friendly with through my parents, agreed to take over for me to do whatever was necessary for the final liquidation of the office. He was an architect from Austria, around fifty years of age, who had been in China since the early 1930s, and for reasons that were not quite clear to me was not ready to leave. He and his wife had no children and apparently had no place to go. I do not know why he would not even contemplate going back to Austria. I surmise he took the same gamble I did and hoped he could ride out the storm, and as the survivor would get command of the ship.

Mr. Hajek took over responsibility for the office files, one of the conditions the Communists had imposed before granting our exit visas, and various small claims that were still pending. Eventually, Hajek did leave Shanghai, returned to Vienna and whatever his arrangements with Mr. Allman were, they did not end on a happy note. To me nothing mattered at that point except to get out. The general situation grew worse daily and Shirley was pregnant. Any further delays would have made our departure impossible until Shirley and the baby could travel, which could mean at least six more months in this hell. The last few days before our departure were harrowing. There were attempts at blackmail and telephone threats. My fears were well-founded. According to a letter I received when we arrived in Vienna in April 1952 from Mr. Hajek, the police came to the house to arrest me shortly after we had left for the railroad station. The charge apparently was espionage. The arrest of a Chinese lawyer, Dr. Ai, the same day would seem to explain what happened. I had worked with Dr. Ai to translate official, published legal decrees and sent them to Mr. Allman so that he could continue to advise clients in the United States on legal problems in China. In the twisted minds of a police state everyone is under suspicion.

Of course, it must be remembered that due to the fact that China and the US were fighting in Korea, although not officially at war, the United States still had the status of enemy number one. It never occurred to me that sending published information to another country could be construed as espionage.

But once again my luck held out, and on February 25th 1952, two and three fourths Hoffmanns escaped from Shanghai.

An article entitled "Communism and What It Will Do To You",[12] which I wrote in March and April of 1952, supplements this chapter and is included at the end of the book. Because it is the only contemporaneous material I have, except for some letters, I have not edited it to avoid detracting from its value as a true description of life as it was under the new Communist

---

12 See Appendix: VOA Communism Article "Communism and What It Will Do To You"

regime. This article was used for a series of broadcasts in January and February of 1953 over the Voice of America, the United States Information Service radio station that broadcasts across the globe.[13]

---

[13] See Appendix: United States Information Services Letter, March 6, 1953, Director USIS Russell L. Harris

18

SHANGHAI TO NEW YORK:
FEBRUARY 1952 – APRIL 1953

IT IS REALLY impossible to describe the sense of relief we felt boarding the train for Canton after the tensions of the last few days before our departure from Shanghai. We had sent most of our belongings to my parents in the US and traveled with only two or three suitcases of clothing. The office boy, Peter, whom I mentioned previously, came to the station with us. In contrast, my university friend, Jerry Liu, the fellow whom I had gotten the job at the firm, sent us a very nice sendoff present but explained that he was afraid to be seen with foreigners.

The formalities at the Customs checkpoint were rudimentary. The Chinese officers turned the suitcases upside down on the dusty ground and rummaged through them. They found nothing of interest and we finally boarded the train on our two-and-a-half day journey to Canton. Foreigners were not permitted to leave Shanghai by boat, obviously the more convenient method of departure. I have no recollection whether there was any civilian air traffic in and out of Shanghai at the time, but if there was, it was not available to people like us. We traveled in a first class sleeper, which was not bad, but we were not permitted to leave the compartment or the train. I do not recall what happened when one had to go to the bathroom, but a Chinese soldier always patrolled the corridor so you could not stray very far. If there was a dining car on the train, it was not accessible to us; food was brought to our compartment. I knew there were other foreigners on the train, but never saw them.

How does one spend sixty hours cooped up on a moving train? We played a lot of cards. The guard was no less bored than we were and wanted to join our card game, but the language barrier was too daunting of an obstacle. Upon arrival in Canton, we were met by a police bus. Even though we had not left the train, our luggage was again inspected by being emptied on the ground. Then we were taken to the police station to register our arrival and from the police station we were taken to a hotel. We were given strict instructions not to leave the hotel until we were picked up in the morning to go to the train that would take us to Hong Kong. I left Shanghai with enough Chinese money for the expenses of the trip, and once we were in Hong Kong I would have access to funds from my US bank account where my salary had been accumulating.

In the hotel we finally could move about a little, and even ate in the dining room, but the night was sleepless. The bed bugs saw to that. In the morning our luggage was again inspected and we were taken back to the police station to register our departure. From there it was on to the train and the last leg of our journey to freedom. Before we boarded the train to Hong Kong our luggage was again inspected. I do not recall the three-hour train trip, but I remember the last luggage inspection at the Hong Kong border and the walk across the bridge as if it had happened yesterday.

As foreigners, we had to wait until everyone else had been inspected, including livestock, such as chickens and pigs that were brought to be sold in the markets of Hong Kong. When it was our turn, the suitcases were once again emptied out onto the ground. A large diamond brooch, which we were taking out for some friends, lay there in the dirt. The border guards obviously did not know its value and paid no attention to it. We were allowed to put our things back into the suitcases and walked over the bridge to freedom. For the second time in thirteen years, I had made my escape from a regime that had made life not only impossible, but threatened life itself. How did I feel? I can only describe the feeling as immense relief. My escape from Hitler was burdened by the worry of the fate of my parents and my lack of resources. This time, my concerns were to get Shirley settled somewhere in time for the birth of our baby and to get to the United States as soon as possible to restart my career.

The accountant who had worked at US Lines in Shanghai, and whom I knew well, was at the checkpoint to pick us up. I can still hear him saying, "You can relax now, you are safe."

US Lines had arranged hotel and boat reservations. The boat would leave in a week and we were busy throughout our stay in Hong Kong. I had to spend some time at the US Lines office sending cables, writing letters and obtaining funds. I still remember asking for $1,000, a sizable amount back then. I was interviewed by the political officer at the United States Consulate about my experiences in China. We were invited out by a Chinese fellow to whom we delivered the diamond brooch and a seven carat diamond ring. He was entrusted to keep the jewelry for our friends until they could retrieve it. I remember going to the hot, crowded races. Shirley went shopping and bought a suitcase full of baby clothes and other necessities. We went sightseeing. I particularly recall the Repulse Bay Hotel, which is still one of the nicest spots in Hong Kong. We were free to come and go without worrying about every knock on the door or every phone call. We did not miss the constant police car sirens that had become part

Shirley & Paul-Repulse Bay Hotel Hong Kong March 2, 1952

of the daily background noise in Shanghai.[14]

We had made the decision to emigrate to the United States. It was a natural consequence of my association with Americans and now my whole family was there. In addition, I needed to go to New York to settle matters with Judge Allman. I never seriously considered going back to Vienna permanently. I simply could not conceive of living among people who were responsible for so much pain and suffering. We considered going to Israel, where Shirley's family had settled, but the reports from there were certainly not encouraging. Living conditions for new immigrants were extremely difficult. I could not imagine how I would make a living without practical knowledge of Hebrew, and knew I could not depend on my ability to engage in physical labor. (In retrospect, I feel sure I would have managed. and maybe felt as much at home in Israel as I felt when we had the opportunity to visit later on.)

Why did we go to Europe to wait for our visas to the United States? It would have been more practical to stay in Hong Kong. I think part of my decision had to do with my desire to get as far away from the Communists as possible. The British authorities also made it difficult to get a visa to stay in Hong Kong for any length of time. It was also a good idea to go to

---

14 Excerpt from first letter from Paul and Shirley to Paul's family upon leaving Shanghai, March 2, 1952: "The terror there (Shanghai) is worse than anything I have ever seen, and if you were not a Jew, Hitler was paradise."

Vienna to investigate the status of a property my cousins and I had inherited from Grandfather Singer. I did not plan to stay in Vienna for any length of time, both because of my fear of the Communists, who controlled part of the city, and my antipathy towards the Viennese. I asked the American Consulate in Shanghai to transfer our visa applications to Milan. The choice of Milan was based on nothing more than a fancy. As a boy, I had seen a model of the famous dome and promised myself that one day I would see this extraordinary structure.

On March 7, 1952 we boarded the *Felix Roussel*, a French steamer, to begin our thirty-day journey to Marseilles. US Lines had booked a suite for us, honoring the agreement for first class transportation to the United States. We had a marvelous trip. Our first stop was Manila. We were invited to lunch by Admiral Giles Stedman, now the US Lines regional Vice President, who also provided an escort for the entire day the *Felix Roussel* was docked in Manila. Old Manila, the center of the city was totally destroyed, not a single wall had been left standing.

Our next stop was Singapore, where we had to repay some money I borrowed in Shanghai, and did some sightseeing. Then it was on to Saigon. The fight for independence from the French

Felix Roussel

spearheaded by Ho Chi Minh and the Communists had already begun. We were ordered below deck while sailing up the Mekong River to the port because of the danger of sniper fire.

We were in Saigon for three days, a rather European-looking city. My lasting memory was the unbearable heat. You could feel it through your shoes and we stopped often to have a drink. Shirley, being pregnant, suffered more than I. Her feet and legs were swollen and we had to buy her new shoes. When we departed, a number of French women and children who were being evacuated came aboard. The ship's newspaper reported that an hour after the ship left port, a bomb meant for the ship exploded. Again, it seems, my usual luck kept us one step ahead of disaster.

Our next port was Colombo, which was also a port of call in 1938. I remember that we were offered to purchase precious stones, primarily rubies, at ridiculously low prices. We did not buy any, not knowing what was real and what was not. It also seemed inappropriate to invest in jewelry, given our uncertain future. We were happy to have dinner away from the ship for a change. The curry we ordered was just too hot for me, although Shirley had no problem with it. On the way from Colombo to Djibouti, I suffered a mild case of sunstroke. Shirley called the doctor and when he arrived he was disappointed; he had hoped to deliver a baby. Djibouti was not a very pleasant experience. Of course it was terribly hot, but even worse, my glasses were stolen right off my nose. We had been warned that this could happen, and it did, while I was concentrating on taking a photograph. I was not the only passenger who lost their glasses that day. Fortunately, I had a spare pair. The place itself was not at all attractive; lots of poverty and people with open sores begging on the streets.

Our next port of call was Suez. We were offered a tour that

Paul in Egypt April 2, 1952

would take us to Cairo while the ship passed through the Suez Canal. We would rejoin the ship in Port Said. Unfortunately, it was not advisable for Shirley to go. The trip was just too strenuous for a woman in her condition, but as usual she did not object to my going. It was a most interesting day. We went to see the pyramids and the Sphinx, the great mosque of Cairo and the museum where the treasures of the pharaohs, including those of Tutankhamen were displayed.

Frankly, I was not overly impressed with the pyramids and the Sphinx, possibly because we were there in the heat of the day. The mosque, with its vast emptiness, was far more impressive. Cairo seemed even more crowded than Shanghai. People were hanging on the outside of the trolleys without any visible contact with the trolley, like a cluster of insects. Our arrival in Cairo was about a month following some very severe anti-foreign, primarily anti-British riots. The biggest hotel in the city was gutted and the atmosphere was clearly very tense. On the way to Port Said, we were halted at a British military post. The travel agency, Thomas Cook, had neglected to advise the checkpoint that we were coming and it took quite a while to straighten things out. Those of us on the tour worried the whole time that the ship would leave without us. I shudder to think what would have happened if we had run into Egyptian soldiers.

We arrived back to the ship safely and started out on the last leg of our journey to Marseilles. About thirteen and a half years had passed since I had left Europe. As we entered a new phase of our life, it was astonishing how well Shirley adjusted to what must have been certainly strange surroundings and circumstances for her. But, if any place could prepare you for a life outside China, it was Shanghai. Its multitude of different nationalities and cultures was an excellent school of life. Many doors in the foreign community were opened to Caucasians in Shanghai, and thus Shirley was exposed to all kinds of social interaction during her twelve years there. One of Shirley's most endearing qualities was that no matter what the surroundings, she was always herself. She was never overawed by the elegance or splendor of an occasion, and behaved equally naturally in the most constrained surroundings. This aspect of Shirley's personality, among others, made her universally popular; I never met anyone who didn't enjoy her company.

When we landed in Marseilles, our first dinner was at the port, where Shirley was introduced to bouillabaisse. She also marveled at the first vending machine she ever saw. We went to a show, dancing girls a la Folies Bergeres. From Marseilles we took the train to Milan, a most beautiful trip along the French Riviera. Our first stop when we arrived in Milan was at the American Consulate, which blithely informed us that they had no visa section and that our papers had been sent to Genoa. We spent two days in Milan. We saw the Duomo di Milan, and I was not disappointed. It was as magnificent as I had imagined. I found out that the opera, the famous La Scala, was performing that night and I hurried to get tickets. I was delighted that I could get first balcony seats at a very reasonable price. What I did not know was that the first balcony is the only balcony because the lower four floors are boxes. The seats were so narrow poor Shirley barely fit into the seat. The performance was Mozart's Abduction from the Seraglio with Maria Callas. At the time we did not know who Maria Callas was, but the discomfort of the narrow seats, the heat, and the distance from the stage made it difficult to appreciate the opera.

On Good Friday April 11, 1952, we went to Genoa. I am sure of the date because so many other people wanted to go to Genoa and the Italian Riviera for the long Easter weekend. The train was filled beyond capacity and I was literally wedged in on the platform between the cars for the entire two-and-a-half hour trip to Genoa. Fortunately, the Italians have a great concern for pregnant women and women with children, and somebody immediately stood up to give Shirley a seat. On arrival in Genoa, we found our way to a pleasant boarding house. Since it was also Passover, Shirley wanted matzah. We found the Jewish Community Center and they gave us some matzah. The American consulate did not open until Tuesday, as Easter Monday is a holiday in Europe, so we explored Genoa, a very agreeable city which still showed some of the ravages of the war. The weather was delightful and one day we went to Nervi, the first town on the Riviera east of Genoa. It was so beautiful and I remember saying to Shirley that I thought it would be too expensive for us to live there while waiting for our visa. Fortunately, I was wrong and we eventually spent nine glorious months there.

On Tuesday, we checked in at the Consulate and were told that it would take a few months to process the papers and that in the meantime we could go to Vienna. So Vienna became our next destination. I hoped to collect some money there from the

Shirley Piazza San Marco-Venice April 1952

property I inherited, and my cousin Erwin had returned to Vienna and could help us with arrangements for the birth of the baby. On the way to Vienna, we stopped in Venice for a few days. I had spent a few hours there on the way to China and thought it was a marvelous place and wanted Shirley to see it.

True, it was getting harder and harder for Shirley to travel, the baby was due about May 15, but she was a trooper. After all, we did not know if we would have the opportunity to travel to Europe again. As I look back, I was not too concerned about how much money we were spending. We certainly were not typical refugees. I also can't remember how I managed all of the luggage. The fact that I do not have any particular memory indicates that it was not too difficult. In 1952, Europe had not yet overcome all of the effects of the War. The dollar was king and help was available and affordable.

We took the train from Venice to Vienna. Anxiety set in when we crossed the border into Austria, which was still controlled by the Russians. My fear of the Communists had not subsided, and did not fully subside until we reached the United States. I was afraid there would be questions about Shirley's passport, but our border crossing was uneventful and we arrived in Vienna on April 15, 1952. My parents had arranged that we would first go to the home of a pre-war friend, Mrs. Wanke, who was not Jewish and therefore had survived the War. Her apartment was quite small, and we would not be able to reside with her for the entire stay in Vienna. Within about a week we rented two rooms in one of the outlying districts of the city. The apartment was in the American zone. Like all of Austria, Vienna was divided into four zones between the victorious Allies. Control of the center of the city rotated every month. Naturally, given my experience with the Communists, I did not want to live in the Soviet Zone. After having heard that the Chinese Communists had come to arrest me the day of our departure, I was particularly careful to avoid any contact with the Soviet occupation forces.

Shirley with Grete & Erwin Lengyel Vienna 1952

It was now barely a month before the baby was due and Erwin recommended an obstetrician who found Shirley was in good health. It was arranged that when the time came, Shirley would go to a very nice hospital, not too far from where we lived. We were very close with Erwin and Grete during our stay in Vienna, a friendship that continued when they came to the United States. They were always very helpful to us.

As soon as possible, I visited the offices that administered the property which I had inherited from Grandfather Singer. As I indicated earlier, the Singers were quite wealthy. Some of the wealth consisted of a very large tenement which Grandfather had bought when the post-war inflation of 1920 had led to forced liquidation of assets by many people. In his will Grandfather decided to bypass his children, as far as this property was concerned, and willed it to the seven grandchildren. We each owned one eighth, except for my cousin, Fred, who received a quarter share because his older brother had died and Grandfather thought it only right that each branch of the family should own an equal share of the property. The property consisted of two adjacent buildings and through some mistake, the Nazis, who had expropriated all Jewish property, had overlooked one of the buildings. Thus during the entire war, the administrator, Mrs. Pecha, had collected rent. Of course, I was in a hurry to go see her and get my hands on the money.

I still remember my first encounter with this woman, who tried to get my sympathy for all she had endured during the War. Seven years after the end of the War, the first thing she told me was how terrible the Russians were when they occupied Vienna and how she and her daughter had to hide from the soldiers to avoid being raped. She seemed to have no understanding at all of what had happened to me, and even worse, to so many other Jews. Like most Viennese citizens at that time, she felt very sorry for herself. I often sensed that when the Viennese looked at me they thought, "How did we miss this guy, who now comes back and flaunts his dollars?"

While we had a satisfactory time in Vienna we were never comfortable with the people, with a few exceptions. I cannot recall the details of how I finally obtained the money, but the available funds were quite helpful, even though my parents had taken some of the money when they had been to Vienna two years earlier on their way to the States. I worked on getting the expropriated house back. There were some laws in effect at the time that made this possible under favorable conditions. Since we were seven owners, I had to get the approval of all my cousins for each action. This eventually became so burdensome, particularly because one cousin was unstable and not always reachable, that I decided to sell the property. I think we finally sold the property in the late 1950s. My share of the profits was nearly enough for the purchase of the cooperative apartment we bought in the Howard Beach section of Queens in New York City in 1960.

We did some sightseeing around Vienna and met with people whom my parents had known; those who had survived, others who had returned. I found out that one of my friends from school had survived, but that he was an active Communist. That was enough for me to know that I did not want to contact him. Shirley's time drew near, and then passed, without the arrival of the baby. On Friday, May 23, 1952, we went to the doctor. He recommended that we go to the hospital the following day to induce the birth. After consulting with Erwin, I checked Shirley into the hospital on Saturday morning. Unfortunately, whatever measures they took to induce the birth did not work. Shirley was in a lot of pain, but there was no baby. At about eight o'clock that evening, I was told to go home. The hospital would call me if anything happened during the night. When I woke up at six o'clock the next morning, only to find that the baby was still not born, I called Erwin and asked him to come to the hospital. From the first day we had arrived in Vienna, Erwin and I had planned to go to an international soccer match between England and Austria on May 25, 1952, that very afternoon. I remember telling him, "If there is no baby, you are not going to the soccer game."

I immediately went to the hospital and learned that the doctor had come during the night and stayed to be available. By that time, Shirley was exhausted and I was a nervous wreck. Erwin arrived at the hospital and had his usual calming influence. He sent me to kill time with the son of very good friends of my parents who had immigrated to the States, Hans Furth. Hans was in Vienna to study medicine and lived nearby. I spent some time with Hans and his wife and around midday, Erwin came to their apartment and suggested we go to lunch. Erwin knew at that point that the baby was about to be born and wanted to distract me just a little longer. When we came back from lunch, I was a father. Given the tense thirty six hours since I had taken Shirley to the hospital, relief was my first reaction. The joy came later, and what a joy! I saw Shirley and our little son for a few minutes, and off we went to the game. Shirley was much too exhausted to want to do anything but sleep.

Paul, Shirley & Abe – Vienna June 1952

On the way, I stopped to send telegrams to my parents in the States and Shirley's mother and brother in Israel. The weather was terrible, raining hard, but superstition has it that to be born on Sunday, and a rainy day, is lucky. By the time I returned from the game, I was more exhausted than Shirley and soon fell asleep on a sofa in her room. I had insisted on first class accommodations and Shirley had a very nice large room. (There was a distinction in hospitals between first class and the ward in those days.)

The nurses were all excited about the Sunday baby and had brought us a cake. Shirley stayed in the hospital for one week. We named the baby Abraham Max, after Shirley's father and my Singer grandfather. Since we did not know many people in Vienna, the following Sunday we had a small *brit milah*, the ritual circumcision of a male child in the Jewish faith, in the hospital and went home. Our life started to revolve around the baby. I was able to get a maid to help Shirley. We had enough money to live in the style to which we had become accustomed. The baby was a constant joy and I was crazy about him. He was really beautiful, blond and blue-eyed and people would stop us on the street to admire him. Abe was always hungry and kept us awake for many a night. People thought we didn't feed him enough, although his appearance easily belied the fact.

When registering Abe's birth at City Hall, I had an interesting experience. It was a good example of the madness of governments and their bureaucracies. The bureaucrat in charge of the desk that day was either French, British or American, due to the rotating schedule of Allied control in Vienna. He explained to me that I was really not married to Shirley because Austrian law does not recognize a religious marriage. When I showed him the Chinese marriage certificate, he balked because the ceremony was not performed by a civilian authority. My first reaction was, well, I married her twice already, why not a third time? But then he found another obstacle. The bureaucrat said that Shirley was a Soviet citizen, and under Soviet law, she could not marry a foreigner. Since the Russians controlled City Hall every fourth month, the Russians might find out that a marriage of a Soviet citizen and foreigner was sanctioned, and make trouble for whomever allowed this to happen. At that point, I got a bit upset because if I could not register Abe as our son, how could I get an American visa for him? Eventually, I was able to persuade the fellow that the Chinese marriage certificate was valid under Austrian law. Abe got a proper birth certificate, and was not illegitimate after all.

In July, I decided to visit the Consulate in Genoa to see how our visa applications were progressing. I had also planned to go from Genoa to London on the urging of a former client from Shanghai who thought we could transact some business. I did not make it to London because the Consulate told me that our papers were nearly ready and that I had better bring Shirley and the baby to Genoa as soon as possible. But first, I had to find a place to stay to await our papers. Someone recommended that I should look in Nervi. I went to an agent and he showed me a lovely apartment up on the hill. When he opened the windows, I was sold. Down below was the beautiful, blue Mediterranean. What a sight! We also had a little garden with an orange tree. I still remember telling the agent that we had a little baby and that we needed fresh milk the day we arrived. The milk was there waiting for us. Whatever the rent was, it really did not matter; I didn't expect to spend more than three or four months there. I was just glad that I was wrong the first time we visited Nervi and thought it would not be affordable.

Nervi 1952

I called Shirley with the good news and went back to Vienna to pick Abe and her up. I was still worried about the Russians and the fact that Shirley had been a Soviet citizen when we married. To avoid crossing the Soviet-controlled border, we flew to Zurich and from there took the train to Milan and on to Genoa. Abe didn't travel well; he cried a lot. In Zurich we were met by a lady with whom we had become friendly on the boat from Hong Kong and she helped us to get to the night train to Milan and Genoa. When we reached the apartment the next morning, I expected Shirley to be as excited about the beautiful location as I had been, but then again she never was one who became overly emotional. I felt hurt that she did not appreciate what I had provided, but I guess she was just too tired after an exhausting trip with a cranky three-month-old baby.

Even with the uncertainties in our life, the nine months we spent in Nervi were in many ways a very good time. Our stay was longer than expected because of another bureaucratic foul-up. In early November, we were called to the United States Consulate fully expecting to be scheduled for medical examinations, the last step before a visa is issued.

Instead, Shirley was taken alone into an office and grilled about her father. As I understood later, the problem was that there was a Communist union leader in San Francisco with the same name as her father, Avram Froloff. This was the height of the McCarthy era and everybody was scared to death of making a mistake. I am sure the people who questioned Shirley believed her that her father had died in Israel in November 1951, but it took them five months to make sure, which delayed our departure until April 1953.

We made friends with our neighbors, a retired English colonel and his charming wife. Years later when the Colonel visited us in New York, after the death of his wife, he gave Shirley a ring belonging to his wife emblazoned with the family crest. They adored our beautiful baby boy and because they had a car, were able to help out with transportation when necessary. A Russian Jewish couple we knew from Shanghai were also in Nervi to await their visas to Australia. I was able to make a few dollars tutoring their two boys and, of course, we socialized with them. I met the manager of the Italo-American Society's German branch.[15] I wrote an article or two for their magazine and also did some lecturing. I can't remember whether or not I was paid to do this, but it was something to keep me busy. We became

---

15 The Pamphlet: Revista Dell' Associazione Italo Americana Di Genova, Genoa 1953, N.1, pgs. 17-18, Shanghai's international settlement-an example of international cooperation

quite friendly with the manager, and unbelievably one day, while visiting her house, found out that her grandfather's name was Hoffmann. From a picture she showed me, there was no doubt that her grandfather was my grandfather's brother. I had heard stories of a great uncle who had gone to Italy and married a Neapolitan girl.

We also became very friendly with Abe's doctor, a Polish Jew, who had survived the Holocaust and married an Italian girl he had met while studying in Italy. When we went back to Genoa in 1987, we called him. He still lived in the same apartment and he remembered us, more than likely because of what happened when Abe swallowed part of a toy while we were living in Nervi.

One afternoon, when Shirley picked Abe up after a nap, she noticed that the little rubber disk that was responsible for the sound from a squeeze toy was missing. After a thorough search, she was certain that Abe had swallowed it. When Abe started to cough and have difficulty breathing, we took him for X-rays. Although the piece clearly showed up on the X-ray, the radiologist dismissed it as a button, forgetting that the child was undressed for the examination. Abe was diagnosed with an enlarged thymus gland. His condition worsened and one afternoon, when he started turning blue, we rushed him to the hospital. The rubber disk he had swallowed had lodged in his esophagus and caused inflammation. The disk was removed and he recovered beautifully, but my opinion of Italian doctors based on this experience, and a few others, remains jaded to this day.

I am sure what made our stay so pleasant was the extraordinary beauty of the surroundings, the good weather and our love of the people, who were always so nice to us despite the fact that our mastery of the Italian language left a lot to be desired. Several visits to Italy since then have not changed my view that Italy is one of the most beautiful countries in the world, the people among the friendliest, not to mention that that area of Europe has provided some of the greatest artists in the world. What would the world be without Roman culture, the great artists of the Renaissance such as Leonardo da Vinci and Michelangelo, and composers such as Verdi and Puccini, just to name a few of the most famous?

Finally, in March 1953, we were called to the Consulate and shortly thereafter, we received our visas to enter the Promised Land. I had no difficulty making arrangements for our passage to the United States through Home Lines, an Italian passenger shipping company, once all our documentation had been approved. We traveled on a relatively small liner, the *SS Homeland*, which left Genoa on April 10, 1953. I was still able to call upon the arrangements made with Mr. Allman and we traveled first class, our last first class fling for quite a while. Except for some rough weather, the passage was extremely pleasant as we looked forward to the reunion with my family. Of course, now there was some anxiety on my part as to how I was going to establish myself in a new country once again. As the Statue of Liberty came into view on the morning of April 24, 1953, our forced travels had finally ended. Although I did not know it at the time, the Promised Land would keep its promise.

Shirley and Abe Aboard the SS Homeland April 1953

19

THE UNITED STATES: THE EARLY YEARS

WHEN WE disembarked, Mother was waiting on the pier in Manhattan to pick us up and take us to Utica, a small upstate New York city, about 250 miles from New York City.

It is not easy to describe the feeling associated with seeing your parents after more than two and a half years, particularly when it was often in question if we would ever be reunited.

Shirley, Paul, Lili, Abe, Oskar, Jack and Licci Utica Spring 1953

There was scant time for emotion as the trip to Utica had to be arranged, and there was, of course, the baby who required everybody's attention. I had a quick meeting with Judge Allman and we made an afternoon train to Utica, about a four-hour trip. Seeing Father was even more emotional for me because I knew he was not well and it was a gift that he was still there to greet us.

I know that I have neglected to write about our families' fates after they left China and settled in the United States and Israel. This was not an oversight; we were in constant correspondence and knew everything that was happening with each other. In my efforts to keep the story focused, I only return to the extended family now.

The story of Shirley's parents is relatively short and mostly sad. They went to an Israel that was just starting to become a country, beset by all kinds of shortages, primarily decent housing. From what I have been told, they lived in trailer-like housing with a minimum of conveniences. The great tragedy, of course, was the death of Shirley's father in November 1951 at only fifty-two years of age from stomach cancer. His death coincided with the long-awaited news that Shirley was pregnant. She was expecting the baby around May 16, her father's birthday. There was no question that Abe would have his name. I have always believed that Avram's early death from stomach cancer was related to his smuggling of ball bearings and mercury through the Japanese lines by carrying them in an inner tube belt around his body. Since ball bearings contain lead and possibly some radioactive metal, and mercury is toxic, my theory may not be so far-fetched. In effect, he was a victim of war, a different kind of victim, but a victim nonetheless.

At the age twenty, Teva, Shirley's younger brother, was left to take care of his mother and he did so for nearly forty years. The scars remained with him throughout his life. I also supported my parents from the time I was nineteen, but my father was there to act as a counterweight to a mother's natural possessiveness until I was a grown man and a father in my own right. Teva served in the Israeli Defense Force and worked in Israel in the aircraft industry. Shirley's mother came to the United States in 1960. Teva came about a year later and worked for Pan American Airlines at JFK airport in New York. Fanya lived with us and Teva lived in a boarding house close by. After four years they moved to Los Angeles, partly for the weather, and a good portion of Shirley's family had settled in and around the Los Angeles area. Teva had a brief, unsuccessful marriage and never had any children. He worked for Continental Airlines in Los Angeles into his mid-60's and moved back East after Fanya's death in 1996 to be closer to us. He passed away in 2003 at the age of 72 due to complications related to diabetes.

My parents left Shanghai on a refugee transport ship that went through the Panama Canal to a Displaced Persons Camp, Wildflecken, in southern Germany. It was a very difficult long trip for them. They arrived in Germany in December 1950 and from their letters, the camp was a terrible shock. I was constantly worried, particularly because of Father's heart condition. I am sure I had some arrangement to send them money, and Mother was able to go to Vienna to get some money from our properties that had survived the War. They arrived in the United States in August 1951 and found a place to stay on the upper east side of Manhattan in New York City. Regrettably, I do not have the letters my parents wrote from their travels since I was unable to take them out of China, but mother preserved the letters we wrote from China and our trip. My letters often reflect the letters we had received and probably tell the story better than I can after forty five years.[16]

---

16   See Appendix: Paul to Family 2-2-52

PAUL HOFFMANN

Fortunately, Father could be admitted to practice medicine in New York State because he had graduated from a European university before the First World War, as long as he was able to pass an English exam, which he did. At 63 years old, this was quite a feat. My cousin, Fred Merkado, who had come to the United States in 1938, worked as an X-Ray technician at the State Hospital in Utica. Fred found out that there was an opening for a doctor and Father applied for the position. Father was hired and early in 1952 my parents moved to Utica. After fourteen very difficult and sometimes terrible years, Mother and Father were able to resume a normal life.

It didn't last long. Father died of a massive heart attack on July 31, 1954, barely two and a half years after having found a haven. Father's generation, particularly those living in Europe, lived through one of the worst periods in history, two World Wars and the Great Depression. And, if you were Jewish, the problems were ten times worse than for most others. Mother was the big loser in this game of life, but with the resilience her generation needed just to survive, she succeeded in creating a life for herself in New York City. We were always very close to her and she got her greatest joy from our two children and my success.

This was countered by the unhappy life of my sister, Licci. I have often thought that if an equal amount of luck is apportioned to each person, Licci's portion was taken from her and given to me. The saying that people make their own luck did not apply to Licci. She worked hard at creating a meaningful, balanced life for herself, Heinz and Jack. Her greatest and all-consuming tragedy was Jack's mental illness and suicide, the ultimate tragedy for a parent. I do not know if Licci ever understood how I felt for her and Heinz. Even before the onset of Jack's illness at the age of eighteen, or that was when it first became evident to us, life was hard for Licci and Heinz. It started with the incredibly tough times during the first years of their marriage in China, understandable given the circumstances, but things did not improve as much as one would hope after they came to the States in 1949. Heinz was sick with ulcers and had difficulty establishing himself in a career. Things did settle down once he found a bookkeeping job with Morris and Schiff, a kosher meat producer in the Boston area. Licci worked as a kindergarten teacher at a Quaker School and eventually managed to study and earned a Masters degree in education.

It was particularly tragic that Licci and Heinz did not have a second child, which could possibly have cushioned Jack's loss a little, but Heinz was already thirty-four when Jack was born, and as much as he loved children, felt he was too old to have another child by the time they were settled in the States. Jack, after fighting a painful battle for many years, took his life the Wednesday before Mothers' Day of May 1978, at the age of thirty-three. Heinz and Licci had just moved into their retirement home on Cape Cod, a dream they had for many years, at the time of Jack's passing. Licci was very courageous for the next few years of her life, but I believe that Jack's death contributed to her showing little resistance when she was diagnosed with cancer. She passed away in 1985 at the age of 67. Heinz continued to live on Cape Cod until his passing in 1996 at the age of 85.

As I return to my narrative and reflect back over the years, my appreciation of how very fortunate I have been continues to grow.

Shirley and Abe stayed in Utica in a small apartment while I went to New York City to look for a job. I lived in a rented room in Manhattan with the same people who had rented a room to my parents. On weekends, I took the train to Utica, a less than satisfactory arrangement for someone as attached to his family as I always have been. Living apart and traveling back and forth was also getting expensive.

The job hunt did not seem easy at the time, but in retrospect it really wasn't that difficult. It took only two and a half months from the time of our arrival until I settled into the type of job that led to my career. One of the problems I encountered when applying for jobs was that people thought me over-qualified for whatever was available. I tried to make use of my connections from China and had a couple of interesting experiences. Judge Allman had spoken to the people at US Lines, for whom I had done a very good job in winding up affairs in their Shanghai office. They expressed interest in talking to me and apparently had something available. However, when I came to the interview, I could see on the man's face that he was shocked when he found out I was Jewish. Shipping companies and banks were not hiring Jews in the fifties. He recommended that I see a lawyer who was singularly unhelpful. I also visited International General Electric because it had been a client in Shanghai, and I had played bridge with the man who was now a vice president there. I was turned down and had to wait another ten years until IGE came looking for me with a job offer.

The job I finally landed, and which led to my career, was with Langner, Parry, Card and Langner, a firm of international trademark and patent agents. They had sent work to Allman, Kops and Lee in Shanghai and knew of me. The field of trademarks was expanding rapidly with the growth of international business after the War and they needed help. I started in their assignment department as an administrative assistant, basically a clerk, at $75.00 a week.

I brought Shirley and Abe to New York from Utica even before I had the job at Langners. In the interim, I had found a job as general factotum/office manager in a small garment district firm. Not long after we settled down in our small apartment in the Kew Gardens section of Queens, Shirley became pregnant again. Although we had not planned on a second child so soon, Jeanie's arrival was one of the happiest events in our life, a joy that has continued throughout our lives.

Remaining in Shanghai had paid off because I was financially independent. Judge Allman, gentleman that he was, paid me what we agreed upon and we started our life in the United States with a little more than $6,000.00 to our name. To put this into perspective, the rent on our first apartment, a one bedroom, was $86.00/month, a newspaper was 10¢, a haircut costs less than one dollar, the subway was 10¢, and cigarettes were $2.00 a carton. I think it is fair to say that in 1997 dollars, we had the equivalent of about $35,000 at our disposal. We had to buy almost everything, from furniture to utensils. But while we had to be careful with our spending, we were able to manage and even afford some modest pleasures, such as movies.

Now that we had settled down I had to start thinking about my long term future. I knew I could not spend the rest of my life as a glorified clerk. The reason I had gone to university in Shanghai was to learn about insurance mathematics with the idea of eventually becoming an actuary. While finance mathematics was my best subject, and I was able to teach the course at the University after I graduated, it soon became clear that what I had learned was barely the beginning of what I needed to know to become an actuary. It seemed impossible to start all over on the undergraduate level and I soon abandoned the idea. The only realistic choice left was to continue doing what I had done successfully in Shanghai. I started to investigate the possibilities and found, somewhat to my dismay, that I had to go to law school and that my Shanghai education would be counted only as college. I investigated the various law schools that offered night school and chose Brooklyn Law School. It was less expensive than New York University and had the reputation of doing a good job at preparing its students to pass the bar exam. I managed to persuade the school to give me half a year more credit for my European high school education, thus cutting my total school time to three-and-a-half years. In September 1954, at the age of thirty four, I had to start school again.

Our Jeanie had arrived in April of that year. She was a real gift, and as if she knew life was not too easy at that point, she was a good baby from day one. We moved into a two-bedroom apartment. Our rent rose to $103.00 per month, but I also had received a raise so we continued to manage, more or less.

July 27, 1954 was one of the blackest days of my life. Father had a massive heart attack while sitting at his desk in the hospital. I was at work when I received the news and was immediately told that there was no hope. Shirley and the children happened to be in Utica visiting with my parents. I took the next possible train and arrived late that night. Erwin Lengyel, who had also immigrated to the States since we had been together in Vienna,

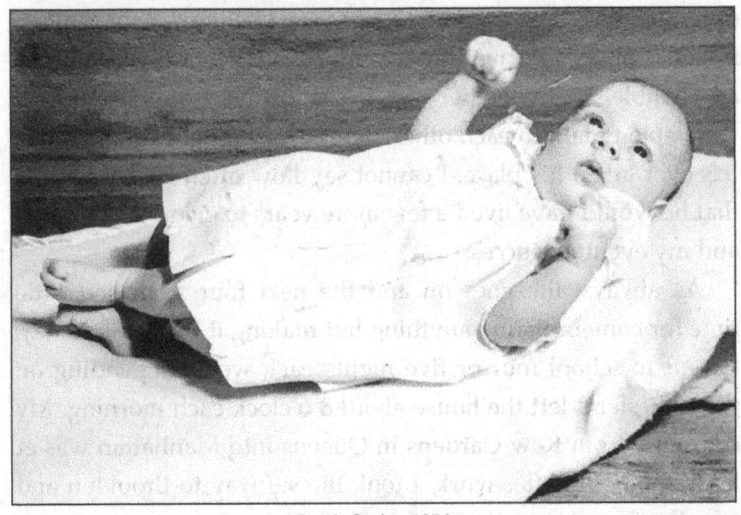

Jeanie Spring 1954

had found a job in the same hospital as Father. Erwin explained the hopelessness of the situation to me. Erwin was with me two years earlier at the birth of our son, and now at the death of my father; a lesson in the cycle of life. I slept the next four nights at the hospital and spent most of each day there as well, until Father died early on the morning of July 31, 1954. Unfortunately, for most of the time he was in a coma or too weak to speak. I do not know whether he even knew that I was there. The only words I heard him say were, "What an idiot I was." I interpreted them to mean that he should have taken better care of himself, but can't be sure that is what he meant.

To lose a parent is never easy, but I was hit hard by Father's death for a number of reasons. I was so sorry that just as Mother and Father had settled down and could enjoy life after the very difficult years, everything came crashing down again. There was no time to enjoy the feeling of safety and the progress of children and grandchildren. Father had often mentioned that he would be able to help me, if necessary, after the many years I had taken care of him and Mother. Instead, I had to start taking care of Mother, not only financially, but also to lend as much emotional support as possible. Lastly, Father and I had always been friends and were able to talk to each other about everything. I think no one has ever taken his place. I cannot say how often I have wished that he would have lived a few more years to enjoy the children and my eventual success.

As always, life goes on and the next four years left little time for contemplating anything but making it from day to day. I went to school four or five nights each week, depending on the semester. I left the house about 8 o'clock each morning. My commute from Kew Gardens in Queens into Manhattan was at least one hour. After work, I took the subway to Brooklyn and usually came home by 10 o'clock at night. It was not an easy routine under any circumstances, but with two little children and a recently widowed mother it seems an almost impossible situation. It wasn't any worse than Shanghai during the War, but now I was eleven years older. We coped as best we could. "We" is the operative word, because without Shirley's patience, understanding and general good humor, it certainly could not have been done. Without making much of it, she understood how important it was for me to establish myself. The future proved that our priorities were correct and I think we were well repaid for the difficult times we had.

While mother was of course a concern to us, she very resolutely took matters into her own hands and established herself. First, she took on odd jobs as a babysitter and a cashier in a movie theater. She eventually got a job in the main branch of the New York Public Library on Fifth Avenue. This gave her a great deal of satisfaction. She was fifty six years old and had

Paul's Citizenship Certificate

never worked outside the house.

The four years passed, and in March of 1958 I took the New York Bar Exam. I passed the exam, and since we had already become citizens, I could now be admitted to the New York State Bar and start a career.

To be admitted to the Bar in 1958, one had to pass the Character Committee, which concerned itself with whether the applicant had been convicted of a crime, held membership in a subversive organization, or other faults that could disqualify a future competitor. I was to be interviewed by a lawyer in downtown Manhattan and went without the slightest of misgivings. Suddenly, in the middle of the interview, the attorney questioning me asked whether I had ever practiced law. Innocently I said "Yes, in Shanghai". The next question was, "Were you admitted to the Bar in China?" I said, "No, there was no organized Bar in China." He did not believe me and drew the conclusion that I had engaged in the unauthorized practice of law, and therefore, could not be admitted to the New York State Bar. I persuaded him that I could prove that there was no organized Bar in China and asked that the committee reconsider my application. Initially, I was devastated, but my luck held out again. A lawyer at Langners, who also was a refugee, had lived in Tientsin, China, had already been admitted to the Bar here, and was able to confirm my statement. More importantly, one of my professors from Shanghai, a Jesuit priest, Father Emmanuel de Breuvery, was now an economist at the United Nations. He had been at our wedding and I had invited him to our apartment after I had found out that he also was in New York. Not even the Character Committee of the New York State Bar, which thought it could dictate people's lives, could disregard his letter confirming that there was no Bar in Shanghai. However, the Committee still made me sweat it out. I sat in an anteroom with other applicants who, due to problems with their applications, had to appear in person before the Committee. Finally, someone came out to tell me that I had passed their scrutiny. It was a fitting conclusion to these events that the swearing in ceremony to the New York State Bar was scheduled on my thirty-eighth birthday, October 14, 1958.

20

AMERICA THE BEAUTIFUL 1958–1998

IT TOOK SIXTEEN chapters to tell about the first thirty-eight years of my life while the next forty will take only one. The disparity speaks for itself as to the turmoil of the first thirty-eight years.

As soon as I knew that I had passed the New York State Bar Exam in May of 1958, I started to look for a new job. I was terribly unhappy at Langners. The two partners who ran the firm had the mentality of sweatshop supervisors. One was clearly a megalomaniac and the other threw tantrums when something went wrong. There were times I needed to exercise restraint not to raise my voice in return.

The job search was not easy at first, but even before I was admitted to the Bar, I had landed two offers. One of the jobs was with Langners' competition and the other was with American Home Products Corporation as a trademark attorney. AHP, which had been founded in 1860 as a pharmaceutical firm, had acquired 34 different companies over the years, ranging from food concerns to shoe polish manufacturers. While I may have preferred another specialty, such as tax law, my previous experience in the field of trademarks determined what I would do next. I accepted the position at American Home Products. On the day of the swearing in ceremony to the Bar, I returned to the Langners' office. It was with enormous satisfaction that I walked into the office of one of the partners and announced that I was quitting, just as he was offering his congratulations on my admittance to the Bar. At first, he offered to help me find another job, but then paled when told I was going to a client, American Home Products. Langners, vindictively, tried to prevent me from getting the job. Fortunately, the vice president in charge of patents and trademarks at AHP was outraged and severed the company's relations with Langners. I did not forget what they did when I became Trademark Counsel at General Electric Company several years later and pulled all the GE work from them.

I spent five pleasant years at American Home, learning the corporate world and more about trademarks. Financially, I was treated well and in 1960, after Shirley's mother emigrated from Israel to be with us, we bought a comfortable three-bedroom cooperative apartment in the Howard Beach section of Queens in New York City. With the children in school, now aged eight and six, and her mother available to help out, Shirley was able to use her typing skills to do some temporary work.

In short, life was fairly normal and in general quite good. Into my fifth year at American Home, I became restless because there was no possibility of advancement. My boss, another trademark attorney hired about a year before me, and I were the same age. I had put feelers out for a new job, but out of the blue, a wonderful opportunity surfaced.

Another fortunate career decision I made was to take some intellectual property evening courses at New York University. One of the courses was in trademarks and was taught by Professor Walter Derenberg, a leading expert in copyright and trademark protection law. General Electric Company was looking for a trademark lawyer in their international division and had asked Dr. Derenberg, who was considered the dean of the Trademark

Bar, whether he could recommend someone.

Dr. Derenberg called to inquire whether I was interested. The call came on my forty-third birthday. I was so preoccupied with the news I just received I got a jaywalking ticket when crossing Third Avenue on my way to lunch. Within a few days I met with Martin Kalikow, the Patent Counsel for International General Electric, my future boss. The interview went as well as all my job interviews have gone. While I still had to meet two other people before a final offer could be made, I knew that I had the job. The offer was not only attractive financially, a twenty percent increase in salary, I was to be International Trademark Counsel, with the implied promise that I would eventually be promoted to Trademark Counsel for the whole company, a position that did not exist at GE at the time.

As it turned out, my career at GE was very successful and fascinating. The highlight of my career was a trademark infringement case brought by General Electric Company of England (GEC) against General Electric Company of America. I had the rare opportunity to handle a case that took me up to the House of Lords, the English equivalent of our Supreme Court. The case was so important for General Electric and we won in the lower court. GEC appealed and we lost, but then we appealed in front of the House of Lords and won. I was promoted to General Trademark Counsel, moved to headquarters and reported to the General Patent Counsel. At 49 years old, I now had one of the best jobs in the trademark field, representing one of the top companies, not only in the United States but in the world. One of the benefits of this case was a lot of travel, if one considers traveling a benefit. For me it was. From January 1965 until I retired in March of 1986, I visited London, England 54 times. Once I was in Europe, I was able to take the opportunity to take care of business in countries where GE had major interests such as

PAUL HOFFMANN

*Paul & Shirley in their Redding, Connecticut home in the 1990s
Tapestry in the background was a wedding gift from Shanghai*

France, Spain, Denmark, Italy, and Germany. The GEC case also took me to Australia three times. Other matters required trips to the Far East and Latin America. Of course, there were many trips within the United States, both to visit GE locations and to attend GE and professional association meetings. Shirley came with me as often as possible. If on occasion I came to a professional meeting without Shirley, I would be questioned continuously about her whereabouts.

In 1971, GE decided to move its corporate headquarters to Fairfield, Connecticut. I consider this move another one of my very lucky breaks. We built what turned out to be our dream house on a wooded two-acre lot in Redding, Connecticut, a small rural town only sixty miles from New York City and ten minutes from GE's Fairfield office. As I write this in 1998, it is twenty-four years since we moved in. We have enjoyed our home here tremendously.

The years in Connecticut have been punctuated by mostly happy occasions. Abe graduated from college and law school and married his wife Jayne in 1979. Jeanie graduated college and graduate school and became a special educator. Jeanie married her husband, Doug, in 1977. Jack's tragic death occurred in May 1978 and nothing since Father's death hit me as hard. It may have even been harder because Father's death was, although a bit premature, an event one must expect in the course of life. Jack was only thirty-three years old. Shirley and I were on our way to Copenhagen that day. As a matter of fact, our plane was leaving New York at the same time the call reached my office. It was nearly impossible to get back to Boston in time for the funeral and Licci told me over the phone that my coming could not change what had happened.

Two years later we were blessed with the birth of our first grandchild, David, to Jeanie and Doug, in 1980. Rebecca arrived in 1981 to Abe and Jayne. Jeanie and Doug had their second child, Cara, in 1983. Abe and Jayne welcomed Emily in 1987. To say that our grandchildren have been our pride and joy would be superfluous. I hope they all know how much they are loved.

In 1982 Mother finally yielded to my entreaties to move out of New York City, where she was still living independently. Maybe the birth of her great grandchildren helped to convince her to move to Connecticut. The nearest place that suited her was in New Haven, about a thirty minute drive, but an improvement over driving into New York every week. She lived there until June 1991 when her health deteriorated to the point that she could no longer stay alone and we moved her to our home.

While life at GE was mostly good, by the beginning of 1985

I had decided to retire at the end of that year. I started to feel bored with the job that in so many ways had become routine. I no longer wanted to be locked into a routine and rules. I had worked full-time since I was eighteen to support a family; first my parents then my own. Forty-seven years was a long time to be in harness. I was also influenced by the fact that my GE pension, Social Security, my Austrian pension (war reparations from the Austrian government), plus deferred compensation and investment income would be enough to continue a comfortable lifestyle. But, during the summer of 1985, doubts about the wisdom of retiring pushed me into clinical depression, a most unpleasant and difficult experience. Although clinical depression is the result of a chemical imbalance plus a genetic predisposition, external events can also play a role. In my case, the prospect of retirement, plus Licci's terminal illness, were the contributing factors. I consulted the company doctor at GE and he recommended that my retirement be postponed for three months to the end of March 1986. Licci passed away just a couple of weeks before I retired. Gradually, with her passing and the end of my career at GE, the depression lifted and I returned to my normal self.

Late in December 1985, I was approached by a very large intellectual property firm, Leydig, Voit and Mayer in Chicago. The firm had recently represented GE in a trademark case. They apparently had been impressed with my handling of the case, but also with my standing in the Trademark Bar, and as a member of the board of directors of the United States Trademark Association (USTA). They thought my name on their letterhead would be good for business. They asked me to join them as "Of Counsel". I informed them that I was not a "rainmaker", the term used in the legal profession for someone who brings in work, and that my strength was more in the quality and quantity of the work I could produce. Nevertheless, they wanted me. As it turned out, they did not want me to do any actual work, or even give them any opinions. I represented them at meetings, which was fine with me. I stayed on the Trademark Advisory Committee of the USTA, which was the liaison between the Bar and the United States Trademark Office. The arrangement was obviously a good experience for me and certainly helped ease me into retirement. Over time, I felt I was not providing any value for what I was paid. Eventually, Leydig, Voit and Mayer thought so too, and the relationship was terminated at the end of 1988.

My final story about my working life may be the singular regret of my career. In the fall of 1986, the Commissioner of Trademarks wanted to leave his position. After some younger candidates had either refused or not accepted the position, I was asked by the Commissioner, with the backing of the United States Trademark Association, to apply for the job. This job is the top government job in the trademark field, a presidential appointment. There is no question that I wanted to do this very much. I thought it would make a very fitting ending to my career. I would be the immigrant who not only held one of the top positions in private industry, but also the top government spot in his chosen field. The first step was an interview with the Deputy Secretary of Commerce. I was assured this was a formality since I had the backing of the former Commissioner, the Commissioner of Patents and the Trademark Bar. The next step would have been an interview with the staff people at the White House and their recommendation to be nominated. While waiting for the meeting with the Deputy Secretary, Shirley and I started to weigh the pros and cons. Accepting the position would necessitate a move to Washington, DC. There were two main areas of concern. The first was leaving Mother, now 88 years old. The second problem was what to do about our living arrangements. Should I live alone in Washington? Or should Shirley and I alternately commute to each other? Should we move to Washington and sell the house, or rent an apartment in Washington and rent the house? Any one of the three choices would have involved a great deal of traveling since I would have to come back to see Mother at least once a month. Then there was the question of whether at our age it was worthwhile to go through such a disruption. There were also financial considerations. I would lose my Social Security and forty percent of my Austrian pension. Unless we sold the house or rented it very well, the financial reward would be rather small.

As I waited for the interview early in November, I saw myself being consumed with these problems, and I am sure, at least subconsciously, I worried that I might slide into another depression. Also, Shirley and I had made plans for our first winter trip to California and it seemed that I would either have to scrap the trip, or travel from the West Coast to Washington. Finally, I had to make an irrevocable decision about some deferred compensation before the end of the year. Without knowing whether or not I had the job, it was not possible to make a good decision.

I had my airline shuttle ticket to Washington, DC in hand. The day before the scheduled meeting, the Deputy Secretary's office called to say that he was busy and delayed the meeting to the following day. I agreed, but then they called half an hour later and asked for a further postponement. I decided that I was tired of being strung along and said that I was no longer interested. Shirley was less than enthusiastic about the move, which would certainly have disrupted her life to a great extent. Whatever the reasons, I declined to pursue the position. Twelve years later, I regret not stepping up to the challenge. It was the first time in my life I had made that choice.

Shirley's mother died after a long illness on February 28,

1990. Then it became clear that Mother was failing rapidly. She developed cancer and it was spreading through her system. By June 1991, when Mother could no longer live alone, we decided to take her to our house. It was very difficult, but the right thing to do for Mother. By July we had around the clock help and the next six months were very hard. Shirley did everything that could be expected from a daughter-in-law, and just like other storms, we weathered this one together. In January we simply could no longer manage, and the doctor agreed that the best place for Mother would be a hospice where she passed away on March 15, 1991 at the ripe old age of 92. To have your mother until the age of 70 is quite extraordinary, but nevertheless, I miss Mother a lot. Since her death, I am the oldest surviving member in both the Hoffmann and Singer families. This is not necessarily the most comforting thought, but the unavoidable consequence of living a long life.

This one bad year has been greatly overshadowed by eleven good years since. Probably our greatest enjoyment has been seeing our grandchildren grow up and become useful and good people. We now have three teenagers. That not one of them has given their parents any problems whatsoever is remarkable in today's world. Emily is still too young to worry about, but it seems evident that she never will give her parents anything but happiness. We already had three b'nai mitzvot, and this year David entered college. He is an exceptional young man and I am so very proud of him. I do not know, of course, how long I will be able to watch his progress but I have no doubt that he will do very well in life. As for ourselves, we enjoy our yearly winter stay in California and all the other trips and cruises we have taken in the last few years. We are running out of places we really want to go to, and to be truthful, we are running out of steam. I did have a heart attack nearly five years ago, and while

PAUL HOFFMANN

Paul, Shirley, Jayne, Abe, Jeanie, Doug Grandchildren Rebecca, Emily, David & wife Erica, Cara Spring 2008

I am doing very well, I can feel that I slow down a little more each year. There is also the fear of the problems associated with getting sick while traveling overseas.

Every story must come to an end and I feel that this is as good a time as any. It's been sixty years since I left Vienna. I look back upon a very interesting, lucky and successful life. I believe that the 20th Century was probably the most eventful century the world has ever experienced. It is probably impossible to arrange the events I have lived through in order of importance: World War II, the atom bomb, exploration of space and men walking on the moon, the advent of the computer and the age of technology, the horror of the Holocaust and the creation of the State of Israel, the rise and fall of Communism and the emergence of China as a world power, the growth of the world's population from less than two billion to six billion in my lifetime, and the incredible advances in modern medicine. I am still astonished by the fact that I can instantaneously see in my own home any event in the world and speak to nearly every place in the world by picking up my telephone.

Has the world become a better place since I entered it? I think so. On the international level there is much less danger of a great conflagration comparable to the two World Wars. On the individual level, the human race, while still engaging in unspeakable crimes, has moderated its behavior to some extent. Gone is torture as an instrument of the law in many countries. Slavery and serfdom, although not totally obliterated, is less prevalent. Many countries have adopted social safety nets, unheard of only a hundred years ago. The speed of transportation and communication has opened and shrunk the world to an extent unthinkable when I was a boy. I am optimistic for the near-term future of the world. In the long-term, there are the dangers associated with overpopulation and environmental disasters.

In writing about the significant world events I have lived through, I have thought about the defining moments in my life and have come up with the two events that I can truly say shaped my life. The first was escaping from Hitler and going to Shanghai. The second, which would not have occurred without the first, was meeting and marrying Shirley. The first saved my life. The second became my life.

I was interviewed by the Shoah Foundation, Steven Spielberg's library documenting the experiences of those of us who survived, or in my case, escaped the Holocaust. My interview serves as a remembrance of those events. My hope for this volume is that it serves as a family chronicle. I started with the history of our ancestors and I hope that our children and grandchildren, and future generations, will continue to share the stories of their lives.

I have tried to paint a picture of my view of life and the person I became. I conclude with the wish that my children and grandchildren, when all is said and done, at the end of their lives, will like me be able to say: "WHAT A LIFE I HAD".

November 1998.

Epilogue

SIXTY YEARS after he first arrived in Shanghai, Paul and Shirley visited China in the spring of 1998 when Paul was 78 years old. They visited places that were inaccessible to them between 1938 and 1952, including Beijing, the Great Wall and Xi'an to see the Terracotta Warriors. They also returned to Shanghai to witness the many changes that occurred in the years since they left.

Despite a couple of minor heart attacks, Paul lived an active life into his 85th year. After his retirement in 1986, Paul and Shirley continued to travel, wintered in southern California and took up golf. Life began to slow down in 2006. Paul was diagnosed with Parkinson's Disease in 2008, and he passed away on March 3, 2010 at the age of 89. Shirley passed away two years later at age 84 due to complications related to an auto-immune disease. They had been married for sixty years.

When Paul was well into his 80s, during a holiday meal, he looked around the table and said, "Hitler failed." What he saw were his children and grandchildren, all educated, all having successful careers, and all having chosen to remain active members of the Jewish Community.

We are quite confident that he would say his greatest legacy is his two children, four grandchildren and to date, five great grandchildren.

Paul and Shirley in Beijing in 1998

Appendices

1. Deportation Orders for Dr. Oskar Hoffmann & Alice Hoffmann

Paul's parents were ordered to report to the dome hall of the Temple on Tuesday, October 24, 1939 to be transported for resettlement in the Polish Territory.

12.10.1939

Mr. Oskar Hoffmann

According to the authority's order, you and your family members (the latter, as long as they have reached the age of 16) are designated for resettlement to Polish territory and your departure will have to be carried out with the transport which leaves on Tuesday, October 24th, 1939.

You are requested to fill out the attached questionnaire in a complete and detailed manner and bring it along with identification and travel documents and possibly 2 passport pictures of every concerned family member reliably on

21.X.39 to gather in the dome hall of the temple, where further announcements will be given and the necessary formalities are made public.

We urgently bring to your attention that under any circumstances you are obliged to follow suit to the summons ordered by the authorities, if you do not do so, all consequences will be attributed to yourself. It is especially noted that an extension of your departure date is not possible.

The Israelitische Kultusgemeinde Wien [Israelite Religious Community Vienna] who has been ordered to implement this action, will of course do everything in their power to relieve the hardships involved. It is in the interest of each and every individual to support the Israelitische Kultusgemeinde in the fulfillment of their difficult and responsibility-bearing task.

Israel. Kultusgemeinde Wien

Attachments

1 Questionnaire

1 Information sheet

Exeat

P.S Other, previously issued summons have become invalid through this summons, furthermore the perhaps carried out medical examinations redundant.

19.10.1939

INFORMATION SHEET

For the resettlement of in Vienna residing Jews to Polish territory

For this action following guidelines should be noted:

1. Every person taking part in the transportation is allowed to carry luggage with the maximum weight of 50 kg. When choosing the luggage, one has to bear in mind that it can only be stored in the train wagon above the seat.
2. Tools and machines necessary for the profession can, if they are not too voluminous, be carried along and stored in the provided space in the luggage wagon.
3. It is recommend, if possible, to bring the following items

2 warm suits	1 spirit or petroleum stove
1 winter coat	mess bowls

1 raincoat
2 pairs of high shoes
2 sets of warm clothing
Shawl
Cap and gloves
(mittens, if possible)
Handkerchiefs
Towels
Foot rag
Working suit

drinking cups
Cutlery
Pen knife and scissors
Washing and shaving equipment
Candles and lighter
Sewing kit
Deer seburn
Backpack
Bottle (thermos)

Snacks and food, as possible (nonperishable food items)

4. Every participant in the transport is allowed to take the amount of 300 RM (three hundred).
5. An elimination of the transport ordered by the authorities is only possible, of
    a. if the concerned is about to migrate to another country; if the person intends to use these grounds, the person needs to provide the respective documents and prove unequivocally that your immigration fully corresponds to the facts. The mere prospect of immigration in the future as a registration with the American consulate, ownership of an affidavit etc. are not sufficient; rather the date of departure has to be indicated.
    b. Another exemption of the participation in the transport applies if the concerned person is unfit for transport. This fact has to be confirmed by an official medical certificate.

2. Wedding Story: This Is The Story of How Paul and Shirley Got Married

Paul and Shirley wrote a humorous recount of events of their wedding day to send to friends and relatives around the world who had already left Shanghai.

This is the Story How Paul and Shirley Got Married

It is not a very original story, but to us it seems so. After weeks of feverish preparations, during which time all participants got a few inches smaller from running around, Zero Hour approached. The last week was spent in various activities such as: marketing, arranging, trying on suits and dresses, not to forget the very important dresses of the mothers-in-law. The clothing situation of fathers-in-law proved considerably less troublesome. By Saturday 7 PM practically all participants passed out. It is reported on good authority that the two main participants in the event spent a fitful night.

Sunday morning came and by special courtesy the weather was nice.

Although the bridegroom was not supposed to see the bride, he heard plenty of her and the telephone was busy all day. By 2 o'clock the final ordeal had started. Amidst general confusion, the participants started to dress and at 3:15 the bridegroom's escorts came to take him to his fate.

The synagogue was decorated nicely with blue and white flags and long before 4 o'clock, the official deadline, a great crowd had assembled. There were all nationalities and people from all walks of life, and even a Jesuit priest. The Rabbi as usual did not show any signs of a recent bath, but it is hoped that very few people noticed. However, the Hazen made up for it with his beautiful singing. The bride was late as usual and the poor groom walked the stage like the proverbial lion in the cage. The ceremony concluded and the bride and groom were mobbed by guests, but managed finally to land safely in the car. It should be noted that the young couple had to wait for the flower girl, because what always seems to happen to little girls on occasions like this, happened again.

The next scene plays at the photographer with the groom nervously looking at his watch and the bride posing calmly *for* one picture after another.

When the photographer released the young couple from his clutches, they sped to the reception, being late as is customary. Not less than 250 people waited for them there, most of them already very happy from continuous trips to the bar. The wedding march, toast, cutting of cake and the first waltz followed in short order and then the party went its usual course. It may be noted that by this time the bride and groom were quite tired but still can faintly remember what happened. In any case the photographer with his snaps helped later to refresh their memories. The cocktail reception was attended by 250 people who consumed gallons of whiskey and vodka as well as hundredweights of sandwiches. There were many big-shots, who distinguished themselves by drinking a little more.

To mark time between cocktails and dinner, a description of presents follows: careful statistics reveal 90 presents collected by the young couple, a dozen baskets of flowers, 16 cables and several letters of congratulations. Cables were from all parts of the world as a matter of fact from each continent except Africa, as neither the bride or groom have friends or relatives in the jungle. (They do not believe in Darwin's Theory.)

Presents ranged from a fountain pen to pillows to a handsome check. Most note-worthy was the great amount of silver (mean people say that silver is very cheap in Shanghai now), there are at least 6 dozen teaspoons and oodles *of* luncheon sets and table clothes, silver vases, etc. Upon special application addressed to the undersigned with a self-addressed envelope and $10.00 a full inventory will be sent.

An hour had elapsed, bride and groom were back from their ride in a car ready for dinner. It was supposed to be a small family affair, and there were about 100 people, thank God not a lot of them belong to the family. There was so much to eat that the servants could steal half and there still was plenty left over, but don't think that this was because the guests ate so little. The band played, but the bride and groom cannot give full account of the outcome of the party as they left... and lived happily forever after.

Yours truly,
Shalama & Paul

PAUL HOFFMANN

3. Staff Severance Letter 2-12-51

Letter from the staff of Allman, Kops, and Lee acknowledging the worsening situation and demand they be paid their severance pay immediately.

January 19, 1951.

To: Mr. Hoffmann
From: Staff
Subject: Severance Fee

Due to the tendency of becoming worse with the world situation, a remittance from America will be more and more difficult. Therefore we must remind you our request that you pay us immediately our severance fee irrespective of whether you will or will not close up the office at this time. If the office will not be closed at last, we shall, of course, return you the payment. Anyway, we wish to hold the money so as to keep us safe from any emergency.

At the outset, we have to remind you that when Mr. Allman was about to leave China, we pointed out to him and to you that time would come when no remittance would be possible and suggested that he deposited some money in China to pay our severance fee in case the office should be closed up. His answer was that the office had sufficient funds on hand for that purpose and that you, being his fully authorized representative, will pay us the severance fee at any time required. You had full knowledge of this and you confirmed your obligation to do so in Mr. Allman's memo to us. In the said memo Mr. Allman also assured us that the office will pay our severance fee as soon as he has consulted the partners as to the amount of severance fee to be paid. In view of this, we believe that you must have a certain amount of money on hand for paying the severance fee to us when the time calls for it. We are surprised to learn from you now that you have no money on hand and that you have left the money deposited in America. Under this pretext you refuse to pay us the severance fee. If it were a fact that you have no money on hand despite of your previous knowledge that one day remittance will be impossible, it seems to us that you must have no intention to keep your words and realize your obligation of paying our severance fees. Furthermore, your delay to cable Mr. Allman in reply to his cable to you recently shows that you did not consider our request for severance pay as urgent and important. You are only attempting to drag the matter indefinitely so as to wait the time to come when you can really get no money from America and then claim that you can do nothing because of force majeure. With the above and your recently saying that you hope for a war or a military control of the office to relieve you from responsibility, it makes us to believe it more true that your guarantee was merely for the purposes of preventing us from getting our severance pay. Our difficulties compelled us to call your attention to your responsibility in this matter and we shall appreciate your payment of our severance fee within ten days from date.

We have to add that legally speaking you can never be relieved whether or not your hope will come true unless you fulfill your obligation. To refuse realizing a guarantee like yours may be subject to a court charge.

We hope we shall have no dispute with you and remain to be your friends forever and wish also to do our best to help you out in other matters. If at all possible, we do not like to be the first party who shall establish a case against you, either in the Labour Bureau or the worse in the Court.

                                                        Yours very truly,

S. Y. Hu	Peter Chang	Y. H. Liu
Gladys Deng	M. F. Liang	吳永興
S. C. Ma	J. D. Chao	趙秋浩
Millie Chen	F. C. Chao	A. F. Diniz

4. Hoffmann to Allman 2-12-51

Personal letter from Paul to Judge Allman describing the many obstacles he was encountering in his efforts to settle affairs in Shanghai.

Shanghai: 12th Feb. 1951.

Dear Judge,

This is to acknowledge your letters of January 30th, namely the one to me personally and the copy of your letter to JML setting forth the facts that I am not responsible towards the staff, that there will be no license unless I am permitted to leave, about collection of contingent liabilities such as Lee Che, etc. I believe that you are being as unrealistic as possible and that if you are going to persevere in your attitude you may not have to pay the staff, but I will pay with my life. Suppose we could find Liu Hong Sung and he had enough money to pay the claim, his first argument would be that under present regulations he cannot pay an American firm. Most probably I would have to go to court against him and even if after many, many months the case should be won, there would certainly be an appeal. That means that after many years we may obtain something, if everything goes right (court cases take a long time everywhere). And that is what I should rely upon to get money? By this time everybody will have died of starvation. You certainly did not have to tell the FRB that such a claim exists and if you will look over the accounts you have on hand you will note that this claim was written off at the end of 1949. This was a bad claim right from the beginning, so why should I be able to collect now. Why are you writing to JML all the time? You know very well that he never answered our letters while you were in Shanghai and that soon after he left, stopped showing any interest whatsoever in our office. I know you had a nice time with him in Hongkong, but he has not even written me a note as yet, to reassure me or use a little of his influence with the staff. I do not expect anything from him in this regard. Don't you see that both he and PFK took advantage of the office and you as long as they could, but when it came to help they simply refused, or rather didn't even answer? Am I now to be left here to pay the bill for everybody?

You say that you do not know what to do with your servants. Just to tell them not to worry. Well, do you think they are children? I have been stopped from moving from the house. Not being able to keep up the house, particularly with all these servants, it being far away and no car, cooking 3 times as expensive as in other places, etc. I tried to move. I was lucky enough to find a place with a relative of my wife where we would not have to pay any rent and where by sharing only the utilities and one boy we could have lived on my wife's salary. When I told the servants that I am going to move, they rushed to the office and had it explained to me that they will not permit me to move unless they are paid off and sent home. Their argument was that as long as I am in the house I must pay them at least chow money while once I am out I may refuse to pay anything, claiming I have no money and that they are your servants. Li's own words were "if we die you die". These are your wonderful servants which you have treated so well. Please remember that I asked you about your settlement with them and you told me not to worry, that you had arranged with them. Now Li tells me that they had approached you for a final settlement and you told them that Mr. Hoffmann will take care of everything. I believe it would have been more reasonable to relieve me of that burden by paying them off and letting me bring my own servants. Now you say, you don't know what to do with them. Neither do I, but you could send me the necessary funds as I indicated in previous letters and as I am going to explain again later in this letter. The office staff also does not want me to move out of the house because they are afraid that it may be occupied and that thus the last possible assets may be lost. Although the license for the car has been returned, the chauffeur refuses to be paid off, and I could not because I have not got the money and even if I had it the first question from the others would be, why is there money for him and not for us? You will naturally ask me what, and who, can stop me from moving out of the house? Well I could force my way out with police protection, etc. but don't think it is wise nor do others whom I have consulted. Also, do not know if the police may not decide to take the side of the staff. Up till now I I had no trouble with the police and no black mark, so I believe it better not to start. You must also realize that sentiments have changed considerably since you left. So you see I am not only not permitted to leave Shanghai, but I am also a prisoner in your house. Please remember that I did not want to move in and did so only upon your request.

You are most unrealistic when threatening the staff, that unless I am permitted to go there will be no money. They are writing you a letter as far as I know explaining that they never said they would stop me from going. Do you really believe that your threat will have the slightest effect? You are promising that if I will be permitted to go, then only will you be able to obtain a license. Well, they want to see the hard cash and not promises. I don't have to remind you of how many people were held until they either paid or found a suitable substitute. To find a substitute is not possible unless the people are paid off, so there we are. You know that you gave me power of attorney, and now you write and cable that I have no right to settle with the staff. They are naturally suspicious of such actions and believe that once I am gone they will have nothing and nobody to hang on to. In so many words, it is final that I cannot go unless our people are paid and that includes your servants.

With reference to the above there is of course still US Lines and the question of exit visas in general because I am in charge of an American firm which is under control. However, I feel that first our people must be settled, and the servants, as otherwise I will really be forced to die with them and that is no joke.

How can I get money to accomplish this? Very simply as I pointed out in my previous letters. Since you could pay Mrs. Spector $800, you can pay her more. Since you can put monthly something into my account, you can put one large amount into the account and leave the rest to me. As soon as I will have your assurance that this is done, or only that it will be done, I can procure myself as much money as I need. It is legal for you to pay the small amounts mentioned in your letter of January 30th. It is legal to pay larger amounts and if you don't want to pay to my bank or Mrs. Spector, or somebody else of my designation, you can give the money to my sister who will take care of the rest. I asked you to do this in previous letters and quoted how you should cable me if you agree. All you have to do is to cable me "Authorize Hoffmann to pay off all staff members and servants with funds borrowed in Shanghai to be paid back by partners later". In a cable to me privately or a letter you can explain that you are willing to see Mrs. Spector, that you have arranged through my account, or that I may designate payment to anybody I wish, which is probably the best way, as it would then be smaller amounts. I know now that this is the only way to relieve me and unless you agree you will have to realize that you are playing with my wife's and my future. Can I live in your house without being able to pay land tax, rent tax, servants, etc.? What will the staff do to me as they do not get paid their wages?

I will have to die with them. How can I support 20 people and from what?

In your letter of January 30th you state that you are surprised that my sister did not contact you yet. My brother-in-law was very ill and they had a lot of worries of their own. However, I believe that she will have contacted you before this letter reaches you. Also, I am sending a copy of this letter to her, asking her to contact you immediately. Please let me repeat at the end of this letter that the situation is exactly the way I described it, that the solution I am suggesting is the only feasible one to give me relief and that you cannot wait any longer and risk my life. Other firms are solving their difficulties this way and you cannot let me down, and if you think that by threatening the people with nonpayment if they don't let me go, they will permit me to go, you are very, very much mistaken and render me only a disservice. Please act in accordance with this letter without delay. If some of the things I am writing in this letter sound harsh, don't forget that I am desperate.

Sincerely,

Paul Hoffmann

P.S. Before sending off this letter I was again approached by the staff, and told that they will file a statement with the Foreign Affairs Bureau that they have a dispute with me. There is the result of your letter and cable. I am not even supposed to apply for an exit visa until they are paid off.

Your servants have been told by the staff that they have received one and half months bonus, and now claim for it too. Also, in previous years they received only one month. Their reason is that in previous years they got presents from you at X'mas and New Years, so you see because of your former kindness excessive demands are being made upon me, and I naturally have no money to fulfil these demands.

You must act in accordance with this letter without fail.

Paul

5. Allman Letter to Secretary of Treasury 2-17-51

Letter from Judge Allman to the United States Secretary of the Treasury requesting a license to release funds to liquidate assets and pay staff in Shanghai.

390 Riverside Drive
February 17, 1951.

To the Secretary of the Treasury
c/o Federal Reserve Bank of 33 Liberty Street
New York, N.Y.

Sir:

I beg to enclose my application No. 1 for license to remit US dollars to liquidate my law firm, Allman, Kops & Lee in Shanghai China. I started the liquidation of this firm in May 1949 when the Chinese Communists occupied Shanghai.

    I would like to arrange to pay the US dollars to some reliable firm or bank here or in Hongkong and have that firm payout Chinese Currency in Shanghai to enable me to complete this liquidation. If possible I would appreciate some such authorization in the license.

    There is a moral and legal obligation on my part to make a reasonable pay-off of my staff and I don't wish just to dump them on the street. None of them are Communists and some of them have been with my firm as much as twenty years and it has always been my policy to look after the welfare of my employees.

    I have a house and lot in Shanghai and must make arrangements to pay the taxes otherwise I will lose it through excessive tax penalties.

    It is in my own interest to complete this liquidation as soon as possible as I will have to carry the staff until final pay-off.

Details are set out in the application attached and any further information required will of course be furnished.

Very respectfully yours,
Allman, Kops & Lee
By N. F. Allman, senior partner.

6. Allman to Federal Reserve Bank 3-16-51

Letter from Judge Allman to the Federal Reserve Bank of New York requesting that they expedite the license to release funds in order to settle claims in Shanghai so that Paul would be granted an exit visa.

390 Riverside Drive
New York 25, N. Y.
March 16, 1951

Foreign Assets Control
Federal Reserve Bank of New York
New York

Gentlemen:
RE: Application No. 1 (your number B-1784)
With reference to your letter of March 14, 1951 I beg to inform you that in principle I agree fully with the policy of our government with respect to China. In fact I suggested in June 1950 that this policy be adopted. In the present case however it is penalizing me and not the Communists, for the following reasons:

1. The Communist authorities require employers to continue wages and salaries until settlement with staff is made and paid. Thus withholding license merely penalizes me since I will have to continue salaries to an idle staff. In addition to all this, I both morally and legally owe my staff a settlement, which I ought to make.
2. Failure to make such a settlement gives the Communists a good peg on which to hang propaganda, They can and will say to my staff and to others similarly situated, "See

these Americans are not your friends. They won't meet their moral and legal obligations to you. See how they hide behind a license in order to avoid same, etc.

3. Lack of license to pay taxes will cause me to lose my house and land. Tax penalties accelerate at an alarming rate. One of my employees, Mr. Paul A. Hoffmann, has been allocated a DP visa to proceed to the United States and must pick up this visa in Manila before June 30, 1951. By remaining over in Shanghai Mr Hoffmann made it possible for three American citizens to get exit visas, viz.,

Mr. H. D. Carl Manager United States Lines Company
Mr. W.F. Whalen Manager Everet Steamship Corporation
N. F. Allman, Allman, Kops and Lee

Except for the assistance of Mr. Hoffmann the three of us would still be in Shanghai and quite likely in a Communist jail. The Communist authorities will not grant Mr. Hoffmann an exit visa until my staff is paid off and I owe him a strong moral as well as legal obligation to pay off the staff without any further delay.

Therefore I respectfully request that I be granted a license as previously requested as soon as possible.

Very respectfully yours
Allman, Kops and Lee
by N. F. Allman

7. Allman to US Lines 3-17-51

Letter from Judge Allman to the United States Lines impressing upon them the ever increasing danger Paul was facing in Shanghai.

390 Riverside Drive
New York 25, N. Y.
March 17, 1951

Messrs. United States Lines Company
1 Broadway
New York, N. Y.

Gentlemen:

I have just received a letter from Mr. P. A. Hoffmann dated Shanghai, March, 5 1951 reading as follows:

The U. S. Lines staff continue their demands that they be paid off. The only practical thing to do is payoff and liquidate. If there is further delay I am afraid that the staff will raise greater demands than called for by the contract. It may be all right to view this matter objectively from New York but remember I am on the receiving end here in Shanghai and receive nothing but indignities and hardship. Ask Mr. H. D. Carl what he went through and conditions are now much worse. I hope that the head office and Admiral Stedman realize that Doong has run away because he could not stand the pressure from the staff any longer. Just imagine what the pressure is on me as a foreigner and I can't run away.

Bialy of the American President Lines is also having a hell of a time. He had to be rescued by the police from being beaten severely. Other firms are trying to liquidate and pay off, but most of these have local stocks and thus are able to do so."

By taking over from Mr. H. D. Carl I arranged for his virtual escape from Shanghai and by remaining on in Shanghai Mr. Hoffmann enabled me to escape. I therefore feel a very strong moral as well as a legal obligation to do everything possible to rescue him. One of the chief difficulties at the moment is your staff problem. Also, time is running against his DP visa which he must pick up in Manila before June 30, 1951.

I wonder if you could let me know if Admiral Stedman has any suggestions to make as to how this problem can be solved.

Yours faithfully,
N. F. Allman.

8. Allman to US Representative Walter 4-21-51

Letter from Judge Allman to US Representative Francis Walter requesting the status of a bill before the US Congress extending the time period for picking up visas since time is running out for Paul.

390 Riverside Drive
New York 25, 1951.
April 21, 1951.

The Honorable
Francis E. Walter House of Representatives
Washington, D. C.

Sir:
Subject: H. R. 3576

I have the honor to request that you kindly inform me of the status of the above bill. I am interested on behalf of one of my employees Mr. Paul A. Hoffmann and his wife. They are Austrian citizens and were allotted DP visa numbers under Public Law Number 555 of the 81 Congress but unless the period for picking up visas under this law is extended they will just be out of luck.

By way of explanation I had a law firm in Shanghai which is now being liquidated by Mr. Hoffmann and by remaining behind to do so he made it possible for myself and two other American citizens to escape from Communist China. I am therefore very hopeful that the time limit under the above law be extended.

Very respectfully yours,

N. F. Allman.

PAUL HOFFMANN

9. Treasury Department License

The license that finally released the funds so that Paul could settle claims in Shanghai and begin to arrange for departure.

Form TFAC
Treasury Department
Foreign Assets Control

License No. B-1784
Date: May 16, 1951

LICENSE
(GRANTED UNDER THE AUTHORITY OF SECTION 5(b) OF THE TRADING WITH THE ENEMY ACT, AS AMENDED, EXECUTIVE ORDER NO. 9193 OF JULY 6, 1942, EXECUTIVE ORDER NO. 9989 OF AUGUST 20, 1948, AND CHAPTER V, SUBTITLE B OF TITLE 31 OF THE CODE OF FEDERAL REGULATIONS)

To N. F. Allman, (No. 1)
Name of Licensee
390 Riverside Drive, New York 25, N. Y.
Address of Licensee
Sirs:

1. Pursuant to your application of February 17, 1951, the following transaction is hereby licensed:
Make the necessary entries on your books and remit $14,500.00, through currency other than United States dollars to Paul A. Hoffmann, Shanghai, China, for the purposes specified in your application.
You are required to report promptly upon receipt of information that Mr. Hoffmann has in fact left China.
2. This license is granted upon the statements and

233

representations made in your application, or otherwise filed with or made to the Treasury Department as a supplement to your application, and is subject to the conditions, among others, that you will comply in all respects with all regulations, rulings, orders and instructions issued by the Secretary of the Treasury under the authority of section 5(b) of the Trading with the enemy Act, as amended, and the terms of this license.

3. The licensee shall furnish and make available for inspection any relevant information, records or reports requested by the Secretary of the Treasury, the Federal Reserve Bank of New York, or any other duly authorized officer or agency.

4. This license expires June 30, 1951. , is not transferable, is subject to the provisions of Chapter V, Subtitle B of Title 31 of the Code of Federal Regulations, and any regulations and rulings issued pursuant thereto and may be revoked or modified at any time in the discretion of the Secretary of the Treasury acting directly or through the agency through which the license was issued, or any other agency designated by the Secretary of the Treasury. If this license was issued as a result of willful misrepresentation on the part of the applicant or his duly authorized agent, it may, in the discretion of the Secretary of the Treasury, be declared void from the date of its issuance, or from any other date.

Issued by direction and on behalf of the Secretary of the Treasury:

FOREIGN ASSETS CONTROL
By Federal Reserve Bank of New York
per pro (signature of official)

The Act of October 6, 1917, as amended, provides in part as

follows:

"*** Whoever willfully violates any of the provisions of this subdivision or of any license, order, rule or regulation issued thereunder, shall, upon conviction, be fined not more than $10,000, or, if a natural person, may be imprisoned for not more than ten years, or both; and any officer, director, or agent of any corporation who knowingly participates in such violation may be punished by a like fine, imprisonment or both."

10. Voice of America Text

VOA Article: Communism and What It Will Do To You United States

Text of broadcast on Voice of America in Italy in 1952 describing Paul's experiences during his last thirty-three months in China.

COMMUNISM AND WHAT IT WILL DO TO YOU
Transcript-Broadcast on the Voice of America-1952
By Paul A. Hoffmann

I LIVED FOR 33 months under the rule of Communism in Red China, and those long and weary months have shown me the slow cancerous growth of this scourge on mankind, a cancer which strangles man's soul, thoughts and freedom.

This article, based on personal experiences, will concern itself mainly with what happens to the individual, and, how man stops being an individual under the rule of Communism, and thereby loses one of' the main qualities that sets him apart from the lower echelons of animal life. I hold that when a man loses his individuality, which includes his ability to say what he wants, to listen to what he pleases, to rear his children the way he desires, to displace himself freely, at least within his own country, and finally to think what he wants, he has stopped being a man. And that is exactly what I have watched being done in China, and what is happening in Communist countries, and will happen to you, your friends and anybody else who falls under their domination, provided they don't decide to kill you first.

The system is based on fear: fear of your neighbor, fear of your friend, fear of the members of your family. You are not supposed to trust anybody, and. nobody is supposed to trust you. You are supposed to report on all your friends and members of your family and they are supposed to report on you. The police make the rounds continually to question you or your servants, and their questions concern themselves with everything from the amount you smoke and drink, to your friends and what they think. How often and when you go to church, if you listen to the radio and to what, how much you spend on food and what kind of food you eat. Everything is carefully noted down and your dossier grows. Distrust of each other, even in the "Party" and Government offices, is the keynote. Hardly ever will a Government official confer with you alone, always together with another official, the two checking on each other.

"No one is without fault, and no one is blameless, except that impersonal monster "the Party", and those very few who control it. This is designed to instill fear and terror into the ordinary citizen. So called confession and criticism meetings are some of the main tools to achieve this purpose. You are of course found to belong to some kind of an organization, as a worker to a union, as a housewife to the organization that unites all the women of a block, as a child to a youth organization. Meetings are daily, or sometimes thrice daily occurrences and some of these meetings are devoted to confessions and criticism. Everybody has to stand up and confess what he has done or thought, said or heard, which may be construed as harmful to the State or to the organization he is working for. At the same time, he has the right to criticize others and the duty to criticize himself. If you state that you have nothing to confess, you must be lying, because how can it be possible that you did not deviate even in thought from what the present "Party Line" is, and this "Party Line" can change from day to day, without warning. And not telling the truth, or what the "Party" considers the truth is a crime. Therefore, you will find people confess to the most unlikely deeds, ranging from having used office pencils to make private notes or even having taken a pencil home, to having thought something which is not supposed to be thought. And thought control ranges over anything one can possibly think of: family relations, prices, working methods, religion or art. I have intentionally left out politics or economics from thought control because only someone tired of living would confess to even thinking about politics or economics. Those are matters not to be thought about except as, and when, directed by the propaganda machine. True, both economics and politics are supposedly discussed in those endless meetings, but discussed really means talked about by those permitted to, and the rest can only assent, but even when assenting, it is safer to use the same words the newspapers print every day, the radio blares continuously, and the Party people use in their speeches.

Here it should be noted that the Communists have adopted a special terminology designed to mislead their own people, but even more so, those not familiar with their methods. They call "Democracy" their typical dictatorship, they call a "discussion meeting," a meeting where one gives a speech, and the listener may at best add to the "discussion" by elaborating on the speech in the same sense as shown by the principal speaker. They call "freedom" the most obvious slavery, they call "prosperity "a state of affairs when everybody just manages to exist.

Politics, as known in the free world, does not exist, as there can be no opposition to the policy laid down by the "Party." What they call "politics" consists of foreign policy and Party policy. The only possible opposition may be to the individual leaders at the lower echelons, opposition to the union leader in the factory, to the manager, and the minor official. Such opposition may sometimes be honest, but often it is spurred by feelings of envy or revenge, or organized by the higher ups to divert attention from discontent, mistakes or mismanagement.

These cases give the confession and criticism meetings an additional use. Everybody has supposedly the right to criticize others, but not the party or its leaders who are above criticism. Not only are they blameless because it is part of the system that they are infallible and god-like, but also who would dare to criticize a man whose one word can deprive you of anything from your job to your life?

Suppose you work in a factory or an office and somebody wants to get rid of you or harm you. He will accuse you of reactionary thinking at one of the meetings. Everything and everybody that is supposedly against the party is termed reactionary. Your accuser does not have to prove you guilty. It is you who have to prove yourself innocent and how can you prove that you did not think this or that? These methods have been used very widely in the two distinct waves of terror which swept over Shanghai during the time I was forced to live there.

The first started in February 1950, and was directed against all those who were in any way connected with the former Government, or reactionaries as the Party pleased itself to call them. They were asked to register and promised forgiveness if they repent and recant. A great number registered as the penalties threatened were severe, with death as the most likely for those stubborn enough not to believe the false blandishments and promises of the Communists. Also, there was always fear of denunciation, which was easy, as the crime of most of these people was that they had worked for the legal Government of their country.

In their fear of penalties and denunciation, these poor people registered and had themselves stamped criminals and enemies of the people, hoping that their new rulers would keep their promises. Alas, three months later they were arrested in a mass purge, which one must have seen to believe, put on trial, condemned and jailed, or shot. For weeks without end, police lorries, jeeps and trucks full of prisoners, herded in and tied up like cattle, could be seen being driven to and from court, to jail or to the grounds of execution. A favorite penalty was the suspended death penalty, execution being suspended for a number of years to be spent in slave labor, death to be remitted if the condemned has acceded to proper indoctrination to the satisfaction of his jailers. Just imagine to have the threat of death hanging over you for years, never knowing when your self-styled masters will decide to execute you because they think you have not changed your mind enough, or probably because you have stopped being useful to them as a laborer, or they are simply tired of feeding you. Imagine the humiliation of admitting yourself a criminal daily, denying everything you may believe in, denouncing everything you think is right.

A lighter form of punishment was a few months in jail with heavy indoctrination and then a few years on probation under surveillance of the people. I know of people to whom this has happened, and that is what it amounts to. In one case, a clerk in a big factory was demoted to coolie. He was never permitted to raise his head or talk to anybody during working hours. His probation period was two years. An outcast in a society of which he once was a respected member. And woe to the man who shows such a convict any kindness, as he becomes automatically a reactionary. The principle is "Who is not for me is against me", and most of the time, nobody knows what being "for" means.

Apart from those sent to slave labor, jailed or put on probation many thousands were executed in this first great purge, and one asks oneself if those were not the luckiest. The second great wave of terror started at the end of 1951 in Manchuria and North China and reached Shanghai toward the end of January 1952.

PAUL HOFFMANN

According to last reports, it lasted until the end of May 1952. It started with an anti-corruption drive, as apparently a great amount of corruption had been uncovered among Communist officials. However, this drive was expanded to become a campaign against the merchants and industrials, as the blame was put on those who offered bribes and not those who took them. To the anti-corruption angle were added four more "antis" namely: anti-dealing in foreign currency, anti-tax evasion, anti-inefficiency, and believe it or not anti- bureaucracy, 'Thus started the ominous "Five Antis Campaign". What the Communists termed bureaucracy had of course nothing to do with the real meaning of the word, because bureaucracy is really the mainstay of their rule. But since everybody hates bureaucracy, they used this expression for the highhanded attitude of some officials, making people believe they really want to stamp out bureaucracy.

As far as the campaign touched various officials, it was a handy means to purge those who were not wanted, no matter if they were guilty of corruption, inefficiency or bureaucracy, or not. One of those purged was the youth leader of Shanghai who with his salary or about US$15.00 per month lived in a mansion, for which he supposedly paid a monthly rent of US$2,000.00. The question immediately forces itself upon the observer as to why this had not been discovered earlier. The discrepancy was too great not to be noticed for a year or so. The answer is obvious. The man was ripe to be purged for reasons unknown to the public. Another official who took the rap was the controller of the American owned Shanghai Power Company who was accused of having embezzled the equivalent of US$20,000.00, and to have become so bureaucratic as not to permit anybody to ride in the same lift with him. Again, that was discovered only after the Power Company had been under control for fourteen months.

However, we are less concerned with what happened to the

Communist official as about the fate of the simple man in the street, the manager of a bank, the owner of a factory, the doctor who owns a hospital, the owner of the silk store down the street, the grocer around the corner and the butcher in the market. It was those people who bore the brunt of the campaign, which eventually was directed against every kind of free enterprise left, outwardly a campaign of the masses against the individual, the workers against the capitalists, but really directed by the "Party" to stir up more fear and more hatred.

The main outward sign of this campaign, as well as of all other campaigns, which follow each other in rapid succession is the posting of literally the whole city with leaflets and posters with the abhorrent pictures showing the various misdemeanors and their penalties, as well as the reward for denunciation and confession. There was hardly a store in Shanghai; that did not have some kind of a poster in or on its show windows. Most had so many that one could not see the show windows. All walls were plastered, and banners stretched across the streets. You cannot escape the impact of it. I got to the point that I hated to leave the house. One of the more morbid posters depicted a coffin with the shop owner three quarters inside the coffin, and his only hope to prevent the coffin from closing completely is to confess. Confession was advised as in the earlier wave of terror, but, of course, the result was the same. Punishment followed in any case. Investigations were made simple by instigating mass denunciations. Employees were promised rewards if they denounced their bosses or colleagues, and should they have taken part in any of the crimes invented by the Communists, remittance of their own punishment. Anonymous denunciations were also greatly encouraged. A special office was opened in the downtown section of Shanghai where anyone could deliver an unsigned denunciation. I myself saw long queues of people lined up to do their dirty work. Three letters of denunciation established guilt without a doubt, no matter if the same person had written the three letters. The accuser did not have to come forward, but the accused had to prove himself innocent. Obviously, this system left the way open to large scale blackmail, which is not surprising as blackmail is part of Communism, where the ends always justify the means. If you have troubles with your employees they blackmailed you by locking you up for hours on end without the possibility of attending to your most primitive needs, and if the case comes to court, the court does the blackmailing for them.

I myself was confronted with an attempt at blackmail in connection with the "Five Antis Campaign", a few days before I was supposed to leave China. One morning, I received a telephone call and was asked to come to the central police station, the place where the precious exit visas are issued. I was quite prepared to return my exit visa, which I had received a week earlier. It is hard to believe, but the authorities take sometimes as long as a year, in my case it was only nine weeks, to issue an exit permit. They then decide at the last minute, preferably after your heavy luggage has been sent away and you are left without anything, to rescind. When I arrived at the police station I found it closed, as during the earlier stages of the campaign all Government offices were closed in the mornings to have time for confession meetings. I called my office, and was told that somebody purporting to be from the Foreign Affairs Bureau had called and said he would come and see me. Then I knew that something was- wrong as the Foreign Affairs Bureau always orders you to come to them. The man came with the story that he had been sent by the Foreign Affairs Bureau to give me a chance to confess to him what I had done in connection with winding up a certain American Company. They supposedly had found out about it, but should I confess, the Foreign Affairs Bureau would consider whether they should take away my exit permit and what the punishment should be. In case I refused to confess, my exit visa would certainly be cancelled. I naturally wanted to know what I was accused of, but he refused to make any specific accusation. However, asking for a confession, without an accusation is a popular instrument of confounding people. I have heard of people being shown stacks of papers, supposedly containing proof of their guilt of something or another, and on refusing to confess to anything being dismissed after having been told that the papers are just papers. But next time, there would be proof. Those who confessed, caught by the same trick, are probably legion.

But to return to my blackmailer, every time he advised me to confess, I replied that if there was anything to confess, I would only do so either at the Foreign Affairs Bureau or the police station, and only after having been told the accusation. He thereupon tried a shot in the dark, stating that he knew the company in question had prepared double balance sheets. This is very usual in Shanghai, not only to evade taxes, at which he apparently was driving but many foreign firms offices in Hong Kong and elsewhere, prepare one balance sheet for Shanghai operations and one for operations including other branches. As this was the case in the company discussed, I explained accordingly. The man was afraid to ask for money, but probably wanted some. On the other hand, while it would have been very much worth my while to pay something just to be left in peace. An offer of money would have been tantamount to an admission of guilt. Finally, he left, leaving me worried and scared. I had a few more anonymous calls before my departure, but fortunately nothing happened. However, while I am still rather sure that the whole affair was attempted blackmail, it may well have been a bluff by the police trying to get at me, as the man was remarkably well informed about the affairs of the company in question. I know several people who had similar experiences, some paid and some did not, without the payment influencing their later troubles in any way.

And now to return to the "Five Antis Campaign" in general. It was carried out by all possible means of propaganda: loudspeaker cars going through the streets, the mob incited to take part, and eventually it took the aspect of a grandiose witch hunt where nobody knew when he is going to be made a witch, and the number of witches increased from day to day. I know of an industrialist who, daily, during a whole week, was taken handcuffed from his home to his factory to confess in front of his whole staff. He was one of many industrialists who had left China before the Communist occupation and had been enticed to return by all kinds of promises and appeals to their patriotism, I remember a prominent banker, openly pro-Communist, who at a confession meeting was begging for forgiveness on his knees with tears streaming down his face, forgiveness for things he obviously could not have done, as all banks are rigidly controlled by the Government. The sub-manager of a large bank was submitted a questionnaire of fifty questions, including such as why he uses a rickshaw instead of the tramcar and why he telephones to his house from the office. I know that in the confession meeting of a large bank, nearly all employees confessed to have dealt in black market foreign exchange involving amounts of as little as US$5.00. I protested that this could not be possible, and was told it is better to confess to some small misdemeanor than not to admit anything at all, as nobody believes you blameless and the pressure on you would increase and suspicion aroused that you really had done something wrong. Thus, nearly everybody confessed himself a criminal, and the hold upon him by the authorities was accordingly stronger.

I remember the incident in front of a neighborhood provision store when a loudspeaker truck drove up, and shouted: "Boss come out and confess. We know that you dealt in foreign currency. We know that you evaded taxes. We know that you are a reactionary. Come out and confess." And this went on for hours.

Is it to be wondered that during one month there were about a thousand suicides in Shanghai alone? The pressure on the individual increased until death seemed the only way out. Hundreds jumped to their deaths from the skyscrapers in Shanghai's downtown section. A friend of mine saw six such suicides one Saturday morning.

During the campaign, no Chinese was permitted to leave Shanghai without a permit. In cases where people had left or committed suicide, their families were held responsible, which led to the suicide of whole families. Never have I seen so many ambulances scream through the streets. I was fortunate to leave China before the end of the campaign, but I have heard that it grew steadily more ferocious, and then suddenly stopped late in June, presumably to give the population a respite until a new wave of terror will suit the Communist bosses.

I mentioned earlier, the blackmail used in labor/management relations and here are a few sidelights on it as seen by one who was in the midst of it, as I suffered my worst moments in Red China being threatened by laborers, and there was hardly one of my foreign friends who did not have the same trouble. The term "laborers" does not only refer to the uneducated worker in the factory or the coolie, but also your house boy or cook who may have been in your employ for as many as 20 years, will suddenly become your enemy. Clerical staff can be just as dangerous as laborers because, while their higher education makes them less violent physically, they have learned better to perfect the mental torture, which is the mainstay of communist blackmail and intimidation tactics.

The labor situation became particularly bad right after the Communists took over Shanghai. The sudden change in currency, the generally uncertain times, plus, mainly the feeling on the part of the employees that now their time had come, precipitated a wave of demands of all kinds, mainly for money. The usual way to handle the demands was by sending a deputation into the manager's office and staying there until the demands were agreed to, or trying to stay that long. It was often a question between the manager's and workers' endurance. But if one of these meetings was called off, it simply meant that it would be continued the next day, and some of the meetings lasted 24 hours, with the manager being deprived of food, drink and the possibility to attend to his needs. I remember the case of the manager of a factory with about five hundred employees who went through several such sessions. One night, he was locked in again, and since this particular firm was our client, I had the pleasant duty to call him every hour to find out if he was still all right and to find out if it was time to mobilize the police, which one could do, but which very seldom produced any effect, except to break the present meeting with the pleasant hope of having the same trouble the next day. That particular night, my client was freed by midnight, after having given in to some of the demands of the workers. If you did not appear at your office, the workers appeared at your home and you became their virtual prisoner in your own home.

In many cases the employees controlled the phone, and did not permit outside communication. This happened to me several times. The real tragedy of the managers of foreign firms was the fact that most foreign firms were only branches of their home offices and the managers had as little power to act without permission from home as an ambassador who wants to sign a treaty without permission from his Government. Permission for the outrageous demands of the employees for payoff or raise in salaries was hardly ever given as the home office could not understand the unreasonable demands and the amount of pressure to which their manager was subjected. Furthermore, business was at a practical standstill: Shanghai blockaded, confiscatory taxes levied, and the various home offices soon refused to make further remittances. To explain such a situation to the workers was useless. The worse business got, the higher their demands were, on the principle that soon they will be out of a job and the firm will probably be bankrupt, so squeeze out as much as possible while the going is good. They claimed that the various enterprises had made so much money before that they could draw on their reserves, but how long; can anybody's reserves last if there is no business? Nevertheless, the workers would repeat for hours and hours the same thing "Money or else". The authorities took the same attitude, not only in the case of demands by the employees, but also regarding claims and taxes, no matter how unjustified. That led to an impasse, which is responsible for the fact that many people in responsible positions are still held in China, virtually as hostages for ransom. Holding people for ransom is usually justified legally by a court case and a conviction, but it is ransom pure and simple, as not only the firm is held responsible, but the manager personally. Assets are not accepted, but only hard cash.

One would suppose that the only answer to labor trouble of the kind described above, would be liquidation, but there the Government has taken the necessary precautions. No business may be closed unless approval by the authorities has been obtained, and at the beginning, when most firms still had some reserves, approval was hard to get. Later on, when even the authorities realized that there is a limit to the reserves a firm-may have, permission to close was a little easier to obtain for firms not engaged in production.

Once a liquidation permit has been obtained you may not proceed with liquidation until you have reached an agreement with your workers regarding payoff. That virtually enables the workers or employees to prevent liquidation, which has been done. Demands for payoff sometimes reach the most fantastic figures. While the law provides for a payoff of three months' salary as a maximum, six months is considered a minimum workers will accept, and the usual is one month of salary per year of service with six months as a minimum, and one or two extra months thrown in as "bonus" for "faithful" service. It seems paradoxical that everybody has to pay more than the law provides, but the law was not made to be enforced, except in the case of Government enterprises, as otherwise no agreement would ever be necessary before liquidation is permitted. But, imagine what would happen if a firm would insist on paying the legal maximum? During the discussion, which will, of course, be the result of such an attitude, salaries have to be paid. Blackmail and threats will be used by the employees, and no help can be expected from the authorities. Appeal may be made to the labor bureau, but with the request coming from management; it will take a long time to be acted upon. If acted upon, there will be several meetings of mediation, and the workers, of course, not agreeing to three months' payoff, there will follow several meetings of arbitration. By that time, at least 3 months have passed and salaries paid as usual, although no work had been done. The labor bureau has no right to make any decisions, only recommendations, so the matter will go to court where it will take anywhere from a year onwards including an appeal. Thus the whole procedure will last at least 15 months, and while the decision will probably be in favor of management, salaries, apart from all other expenses to keep the office open, have been paid during those 15 months, and that is why nobody ever tried to fight it out in court. Not to speak of the unpleasantness of the situation, blackmail, threats, and the impossibility to leave China.

Very often the labor bureau will not help at all, by even attempting to arbitrate or forwarding the case to court. A friend of mine, a manager of a small firm, applied to the labor bureau as his last employee made outrageous demands. The first question he was asked by the mediator was, "How much do you want to pay?" When he replied, "the legal allowance", the mediator just said, "But this is impossible, and what do you really want to pay?" That went on for several hours at several meetings and at the end my friend paid just a little less than had originally been demanded. The mediator had persuaded the employee to accept this amount in order to give the proceedings a semblance of legality, which they were obviously devoid of.

Your servants have a better method of blackmail. Just before you are leaving, preferably only two days before, they will spring their demands on you. You don't have to agree, and if the demands are too outrageous you will probably be awarded judgement because the authorities are less partial to servants than to workers, but in the meantime, you will have missed your train and boat, as you cannot leave until everything is settled. So naturally, you would rather pay.

The question that forces itself immediately into the foreground is, what happens to the man who cannot pay? The answer is simple. He goes to jail. I was as near it, as I would ever like to be, whilst the executive of a large American firm was jailed for eleven days until the money arrived to pay his staff. The cases of those having home offices are not too bad, as in the long run the home office will pay to save its man, but the small independent merchant or the manager of a limited liability company, particularly if the shareholders are outside of China, is having the worst of it. He goes to jail if he cannot pay, and while he may be released after a time, his liability continues and he may not leave China. Business being non-existent, one can well imagine the position one can get into, as soon as his own resources are eaten up.

The unreasonableness of employees and the authorities in general is at times unbelievable. When the United States Government froze Chinese funds in December 1950, most American firms, including the two I managed, were caught without cash, and in many cases, after all local assets such as cars, furniture and even wastepaper were disposed of, were unable to meet their obligations. I will mainly confine myself to my personal experiences, but a nearly identical story can be repeated by any one of the managers of American firms in Shanghai. The attitude taken by the staff, as well as by the authorities, was uncompromising. We have to continue to fulfill the company's obligations, and that we as individuals will be held responsible. Therefore, it was not only implied, but often said, that the freezing order, obviously a high level policy decision, was only designed to defraud the Chinese people of their rightful dues. This line of thought had as a consequence that every court action taken for default in payment of salaries, severance pay, taxes or other obligations was made a criminal case, although the obligation was never anything but a civil one, if an obligation at all, by legal standards as accepted in the free world. It was more than once hinted to me that not only was the freezing an attempt to defraud Chinese claimants in general, but that I personally was responsible for this state of affairs. I may have felt flattered at the importance attributed to me in being able to take such important political decisions, but that was certainly small consolation. I am sure that our predicament was very well understood, but admitting our inability to do anything about it would have been tantamount to admitting force majeure, and that was the last thing these people wanted to do. Force majeure does not seem to exist in their legal conception, or they were just unwilling to admit it in the case of Americans in particular and foreigners in general, as despite their inherent lawlessness they always strive, by the most devious means, to give their actions a coating of legality.

Well, here I was, with fifty-odd employees in two offices and no money to pay salaries, not to speak of rent, taxes or other expenses. And my troubles were comparatively small as others had many more employees and obligations. Fortunately, one group of my employees had signed a contract several months before specifying how much they would have to be paid in case the office would be closed, the necessity of which was even recognized by the authorities in view of the impossibility of doing business under prevailing conditions. Thus, fortunately for me, the discussions I was to have were only confined to when and how to pay. Immediately, the freezing order had gone into effect, my home office started procedures to obtain permission from the Treasury Department to pay off Shanghai obligations, and had confirmed by cable and letters that it would stand by its obligations to the letter of the agreement, but that obtaining the permission to send the money would take some time, probably several months.

One would think that the employees, assured of their benefits, which were very generous, would have enough sense to take a quiet and reasonable attitude. But, no, that would have been contrary to the spirit of the times. And what was still more aggravating, was that these were not uneducated workers, but highly paid clerks who had received a good education. Also, they had been with the company for many years, and had received salaries and general treatment far above that usually accorded employees of that type. I noticed that those who had the best education made the most trouble and were the actual driving force behind the whole gang, which may be explained by the fact, that they being most unsure of their position under the new regime, wanted to jump on the bandwagon, and thought that by making themselves leaders in the "fight" against capital, they would absolve themselves from possible past actions. I am happy to know that this scheme hardly ever works, and usually these miniature leaders are cast aside once their usefulness has ended.

Thus the "fight," which actually was no fight, as nobody had anything to fight about, started, but everything from winning a sports event, to raising production one percent, or saving ten pencils a month is termed a "fight' in the peace proclaiming Communist states. They came to the office every day, although I had offered them to go out and look for other jobs, without it affecting their benefits, if only they would leave me alone and. let matters take their course. No, they rather preferred not to work and make life miserable for me. About two to three times a week, at least twenty of them would barge into my office, which was too small for eight people, and ask me when I would pay them. Obviously, my reply was standard: "When the money arrives." Their standard demand was, "We want to be paid immediately and you must pay." The sum involved was much too large for the average individual, even if he had not been plagued by Government restrictions, and so we just sat across from each other for hours, repeating in intervals the same thing, I, of course, not being permitted to leave the room for any purpose whatsoever, and cut off from any outside communication. Fortunately for me, they also used to get tired of the game after anywhere from three to five hours of bothering and baiting me, and finally would make a very clever suggestion: "You must send a cable to the head office to ask them to send the money." Cables and mail are very expensive in Communist China, probably to milk those who still have the audacity to correspond with foreign countries. My funds were getting low and sending a few cables a week was getting difficult. However, my refusal would be of no avail. They would keep me locked up until I had sent a cable and most of the time with their wording. They would argue over every word, and not because it mattered or because they hoped that it would produce results, but solely to show their power in being able to dictate to me what to do. I still refuse to admit that they were dumb enough to believe that cables would influence anybody, particularly since the head office had soon guessed that all these cables were sent under pressure and not of my own free will. They must have understood that the decision lay with the American Government. God knows, I explained it often enough and that there was nothing they would do to me, or I could do, would speed up matters in any way. But why not be cussed if possible, and they were certainly spurred on by their Communist organizers, who afterwards were able to say, and did say, as I heard myself, "You see without our pressure nothing would have been achieved. We are the ones to thank for that you received your money." However, in this nice piece of overstatement and lying, the main point was left out. Namely, that without Communists these people would still have their very good jobs, assured for as long as they would give satisfaction. And, I believe, creating all these troubles is part of the tactic to make people forget this paramount fact. Those who do not forget, or do not pretend well enough that they did, are being sent to a place where they will forget.

When the employees realized that they would make no

headway this way, they took the case to the labor bureau accusing me of withholding their salaries. Again, you can see the obvious lie. I neither withheld nor refused to pay salaries. I was temporarily unable to pay. The labor bureau in Shanghai is a collection of shacks, freezing cold in winter, and hot like the dungeons under the lead roofs of Venice, in summer. These shacks are each furnished with one long table and benches without a back, so that you are as uncomfortable as possible. One would hope that this would shorten meetings, but no, the longer the merrier, even if there is nothing to talk about, like in my case, but after all, every meeting is a fight "against capital" and having spent an afternoon "fighting capital" is a laudable action. When the arbitrator realized that there was nothing to be had from me, he transferred the case to court and so I started my pilgrimages to court. Considering that I had also other court cases thrown at me, about which I will write when I write on Communist justice and courts, I became a. regular habitué at court.

The argument at court did not vary in any way from the arguments with the staff alone, which even continued while the case was under consideration by the labor bureau or the court. I was treated as a. criminal who willfully withheld their just dues from employees. No amount of cables proving that the decision was even out of the hands of the home office, no pleading that the situation was due to Governmental action, produced any result. I was asked to pay and that was that. The judge tried to persuade me to sign that I would pay at a certain date, but I did not fall into this trap. Having signed such a promise you must carry it out, no matter what happens, and not living up to it, means going to jail without further delay. Thus matters dragged along until the money was received, and then I had my most fantastic experience.

One would have thought that once that cable arrived, that the

Treasury license had been granted, and that the money would be remitted in a few days, it took some time to arrange for banking as all remittances had to he arranged via Hong Kong, the staff would be happy and satisfied, so much more satisfied, as one part of the money had arrived earlier, and I had been able to pay salaries up to date. Oh no! Now they wanted to be paid everything immediately. They locked me in at the office and demanded that I pay at once their severance allowance. The argument that they had been paid up to date, that in accordance with the terms of the agreement they should receive monthly salaries for three months more and only then be paid severance pay, and that accordingly I owed them nothing, were of no avail. Either I agreed to pay everything at once, or I would not leave the office unharmed was their attitude. They attempted to beat me; tried to make me drink a spittoon, lock me into a box. When they saw that all this did not help, they started to bargain that I should sign an agreement that I will pay them within three days. I knew that I was unable to do so, and while I believed I should be able to pay in a week, I held out for two weeks. I must repeat that at this stage they had been paid in full and that I did not owe them one cent. The leaders probably knew that, and that in any case, full settlement would be made within a week or two, but for purposes of their own, had organized the whole show.

After six hours of this hell, my wife appeared with the police like a saving angel. My wife always knew where I went, and if I did not call her at certain regular intervals she was to try and get the police. She had tried several times to reach me, and always hearing the phone slammed, she knew something serious was happening. One would hope that the police would understand that I did not owe anything and was held illegally, but while telling the workers they had no right to lock me in, the workers denied it and said we had just been discussing matters. The police took the side of the employees. I could never say that I was threatened and pushed around, as all the workers, to a man, would have denied it and branded me a liar who insults the Chinese people. Whereupon, I would have been forced to apologize to the very same employees. The blandness with which these people will lie, and when I say "these people" it must be applied to the whole system, and all those who profess to believe in it, is unbelievable at times. One always has to keep one's temper, as the slightest show thereof, or the words "you are wrong", or "this is unreasonable", are construed as an insult to the Chinese people. They, as Communists, are never wrong, never unreasonable. This is, of course, solely another way of showing you their power and getting you down.

After further discussion with the police, I managed to obtain twelve days grace, but I had to sign an undertaking that I will pay on time. Well, the money arrived in time, and thus there was still a happy ending to the story, but to show the attitude of the labor bureau I will tell one more occurrence in connection with these employees.

The labor bureau has to approve every cent paid to wage earners, and when I wanted to pay the chief accountant of the company, who, while naturally closely connected with management, was an employee with no power of attorney and had been included in the original agreement concluded with the staff and approved by the labor bureau. The official of that same labor bureau now refused to give me permission to pay him. It was not his money, nor could he have any interest in the matter. He just refused. Several meetings ensued as I wanted to help the one loyal employee I had had, but no result. Finally, thoroughly disgusted, I asked the labor bureau official, "Well suppose he was a manager, don't managers also eat?" The reply was a flat "No". This one "no" explains more about Communism than many treatises and speeches. It implies clearly that anybody who does not suit them, has no right to eat and live., and their mass killings and mass purges prove the truth of this implication.

While in my case a valid agreement, which while obtained under pressure, was still legal, constituted the background for the demands, I know of cases where workers discharged anywhere from 1941 onwards, would suddenly reappear and demand either re-employment or severance pay. In one case, a foreign company, one or our clients, had leased its empty factory to a Chinese group who operated the factory for two years, discharged its workers in 1948, and handed the property back to our client. In 1950, the workers appeared at the office of the representative of our client, whose sole connection with the company was that he had been asked by the proprietor to watch the building, since he himself had left Shanghai. They demanded no less than reemployment, or compensation amounting to many tens of thousands of dollars. They followed him around the street, punctured the tires of his car, and in general made a terrible nuisance of themselves. The fact that they were never employed by the company did not matter to them. There was the possibility to blackmail a foreigner and that chance must be taken. I presume, the Chinese for whom they had worked had disappeared. There were several such cases, some of which even went to court and were fought through all instances, when one would think the court would throw them out at the first hearing.

This lawlessness of laborers and employees could of course never prevail, unless the courts, or the travesties of courts, and the so called justice practiced in a Communist state would favor blackmail, lying and perjury, as long as it is in accordance with present aims of the Government. Accordingly, there can be no justice in a Communist state. Law is what suits the policy of the day and may be changed from day to day. The fact that there is no law, and if there is a written law on a certain subject, its interpretation can be changed from day to day, is probably the most sinister aspect of Communism. If you are involved in a civil case, you do not know what law will apply to you, or how it will be applied, as the following case will show.

A tax was levied on certain types of companies in the same business. This tax was considered unjust and protests were lodged, which stalled issuance of tax bills for several months. Finally, one of my clients received his tax bill with a retroactive fine added to it. Since tax fines are at the unbelievable rate of one percent a day, the fine more than doubled the bill which had been sent out four months too late. My client paid the original tax and asked me to write a petition for him, requesting to have the fine waived, as he could not possibly pay a tax under dispute until it was assessed. The petition was rejected and the manager of this firm is still in Shanghai, since he refused to pay this unjust fine. Two months later, one of the firms I was managing, doing the same business, received its tax bill again with the fine added to it. Having no hope of success, but bound to do my duty, I took the petition I had written for my client, altered amounts and name of the firm and sent it to the tax bureau. Imagine my surprise when two weeks later I received a letter waiving the fine. It must be stressed again that the two cases were absolutely identical.

In another more flagrant case of injustice, I was unfortunately one of the participants. The firm I was representing had delivered some cargo ordered by a Chinese Nationalist Government agency in Shanghai, before the Communist took over, to that same agency in Taiwan. But the bills of lading had by mistake been sent to Shanghai and fallen into the hands of the Communist successors of that agency. Not only the Company, but I personally was sued for delivery of the cargo. Civil and criminal actions were filed against me, despite the fact that instructions to deliver the cargo to Taiwan had not been given in Shanghai. As a matter of fact, without the knowledge of the Shanghai office, and that at the time the instructions were given, I was not even connected with the company. While it is a fundamental principle of criminal law that any criminal suit must be preceded by a criminal act, not so according to Communist justice. Criminal action is brought whenever it suits their designs in a particular case, and in my case they probably brought criminal action to increase pressure on me, and thus indirectly on my head office. I will not go into the merits of the case, but, while according to the bill of lading, my maximum liability could have been $500 per package. There were 6 packages altogether. Claim was brought and finally judged according to market value in contravention of the simplest tenets of the law of contracts. Furthermore, similar cases had previously been judged; one according to the provisions of the bill of lading, the other one according to invoice value. One more proof that you may never know by what standards you will be judged. The reason for market value being demanded was due to the fact that with no cargo coming into Shanghai, market values were as much as 6 times over invoice value, and no matter what law or international custom requires, one tries to get as much as possible. A clear instance of blackmail, as practiced by the court itself, as again I could not leave China until I had paid up this absurd judgment.

However, the most unbelievable thing happened at one or the last hearings in this case. Actually, instructions to ship to Taiwan, instead Shanghai had been given by the New York office of the shipper, a Chinese firm with its head office in Shanghai. The bill of lading showed that this firm had a New York office and the invoice, copy of which had been sent to me by the claimant, was also issued by the shipper's New York office. I had accordingly tried to shift the claim by contesting in several hearings that the

Shanghai manager of the shipper had handed the bill of lading to the claimant, while his New York office had given instructions to ship somewhere else. I asked that the Shanghai manager of that firm be subpoenaed to testify, but of no avail. The judge told me, it was up to him to decide if a witness should be called. The judge is prosecutor, jury and when it pleases him, even defense attorney, and all rolled in one. There are no procedural rules whatsoever, and neither as plaintiff or defendant does one have any specific rights. To speak of "habeas corpus" in a Communist state would be the worst kind of irony. Once a defendant, you have no rights, except those which the judge may or may not decide to grant you. No possibility to ask for an adjournment to obtain evidence or prepare a defense. The judge decides when to adjourn, or not at all, and to return judgment at the first hearing. No possibility to raise any objections to procedures or statements in court.

Accordingly, I was confronted with the witness I had asked for in several hearings, at the last one. The judge asked him: "Do you have an office in New York?" To my great surprise the answer was, "No". I pulled out my documents, protested, but the only effect all this had was that the judge asked the same question again, and the answer was again, "No". I just gasped. Thereupon the judge dismissed the witness. The hearing took its course, and I was eventually condemned to an outrageously high amount. This was such a flagrant case of perjury, it can hardly be called perjury because it was too blatant a lie in the face of overwhelming written evidence, to be even attempted in any but a Communist court. In my case, and in several other cases, the decision had been taken long before the case was ever brought to court. As a foreigner, and representing an American firm, I was, right or wrong, to be made to pay the maximum and the rest was just a sham, which was engineered solely to give blackmail a coat of legality.

The system of courts in China as practiced after the Communists took over is designed to rob you of those liberties that were fought for, for hundreds of years; the right to a defense counsel, a fair trial and a law that will assure beforehand a maximum and minimum penalty. The right to defense counsel was abolished immediately when the Communists took over, by forbidding the practice of law. Civil or criminal case, you must plead yourself without the benefit of expert advice. There is no fixed period within which you have to be brought to trial, no possibility to communicate with anyone once you have been arrested. Nobody knows where you are held, nobody knows for what you are held, unless arrested in flagrante delicto. However, the more common crimes, such as stealing, robbery and murder are seldom punished by death, as long as the criminal's political past is clean. But in cases of very dastardly murders, the case is given a political aspect, such as accusing the murderer of being a foreign agent, a reactionary, or whatever may be the most fitting designation in the particular case. Thereby the public is led to believe that only non-Communists commit crimes. Also, in general, ordinary crimes are being kept out of the news to give the impression that none are committed.

The judge must be a trained Communist, but not necessarily a student of law. Many judges appointed right after the Communists took over, were young boys who had studied law for a few years, but had spent most of their time in Communist activities. Court hearings are very informal. Anybody, even if not asked, or not even a direct party to the dispute, may speak. The judge has unlimited power. He may not only judge the case brought before him, but also anything under dispute in relation thereto.

I remember one case where one party had brought suit against eviction. In the course of the proceedings, it became apparent that the whole statue of the property was not clear, that rent had not been paid, that one of the owners of the property had died without leaving a will. When judgment was finally rendered, people against whom no suit had been brought were condemned to pay rent. I was one of them, although I had never been in court and was in the process of negotiating an amicable settlement. The part of the property which was apparently ownerless was adjudicated to the Government and the agent who had previously received rent under a contract which was still valid, was condemned to pay the rent previously received to the Government. Another contract was set aside and the rent altered. With one word the whole problem was solved. While this system may seem practical, the inherent dangers are immediately apparent. You are at the mercy of the court, without summons and, without ever having had a chance to present your case. A friend of mine was called as a witness in a civil case and left the court as the defendant, being eventually condemned to pay.

However the worst feature of Communist justice is the peoples' trial applied to cases of supposed political importance, such as the trials of former landlords who allegedly had suppressed the tenant and the trials of so called reactionaries. A crowd of anywhere from ten to twenty thousand is commanded into a stadium, and the poor accused are led into the arena, bound like cattle, forced to kneel and then the accusations start. Any number of accusers, probably most of them hired and instructed by the "Party", come forward and accuse the victims of the most hideous crimes. Anybody who knows mass psychology will understand that the verdict of the crowd can only be one, "death", and the Communist butchers pride themselves that they are dispensing justice since as many as twenty thousand people agreed on the death penalty. That the poor victims are often beaten stoned and spat upon, is only natural. These people's trials are broadcast over all radio stations, and all shops that have radios are forced. to turn them on at full blast, as well as the various loudspeakers set up on the streets and in the offices are going their loudest. No matter how much you may want to, you cannot escape the impact of the trial. It may last as long as 8 hours, and I have been forced to listen to it all through loudspeakers across the street. While I do not understand Chinese, it was one of the most awful experiences I ever had, as one could discern very well what happened, and when the crowd howled for the death of the victim. The executions themselves are also made a mass amusement. I have seen people driven in open trucks to the execution and the crowd applauding as they passed. The newspapers, even the one English language newspaper printed by the Communists, will give accounts of the executions, how many people attended and how they applauded every salvo.

I have set out to show what Communism will do to you as an individual: how it will warp your thinking and how it will make an animal of the herd out of you, whose life is not safe at any time, whose time is not his own, and whose thoughts are never supposed to be his own. While I had to draw heavily on personal experiences and have shown mostly the troubles one can have, not only those who have the troubles must be pitied, but still more the mass, which apparently give you the troubles. It is they who have lost their individuality, and are, through constant pressure and propaganda being made to lose any semblance of free life, and all those things that freedom loving people have died for, for centuries, and prize as their natural rights.

PAUL HOFFMANN

11. Information Services Letter, March 6, 1953

Letter from Russell L. Harris, Director of the USIS, to Paul describing the positive response to the broadcast and repeat broadcasts and plans for future use.

UNITED STATES INFORMATION SERVICE
PIAZZA PORTELLO, 6 - GENOA
TELEPHONE 23259

March 6, 1953

Mr. Paul Hoffman,
Via S. Ilario 38/1,
Genova-Nervi.

Dear Mr. Hoffman:

Rome has written us that the Department of State was very pleased with your tape recordings and has begun to make very good use of them. The tape was edited and used on a special half hour broadcast in the European English Service on January 12. It was also edited into three quarter programs for the series "Spotlight on the Pacific" which was broadcast to the Far East on January 19, 26, and February 2. The English to the Near East Service is planning a program built around your tape recording. Requests have also been received from other branches for discs made from your tape to be used locally.

The Department of State has asked us whether you would be able to do another recording in Italian for use on the Italian shortwave broadcasts.

Many thanks for your cooperation and contribution to our program, which you can see has been much appreciated all around.

Sincerely yours,

Russell L. Harris
Director USIS
Liguria

12. The Pamphlet: Revista Dell' Associazione Italo Americana Di Genova

Article written by Paul in Italy in 1953 describing life in Shanghai prior to 1949.

Shanghai's international settlement an example of international cooperation

Once upon a time there was a city, governed by an international body, nearly without any taxes, without any restrictions on entrance or departure, but orderly and an example for many other city administrations.

This modern fairytale was Shanghai's international settlement. Fairy tales do not concern themselves with the "why", but tell us of the miracles that happened and how, and so we only concern ourselves with the facts that made this experiment work, an exceptional example of international cooperation and so successful it not only brought its inhabitants a standard of living far above that, prevailing in the country surrounding it, that not only a haven of safety from the upheavals of its mother country, but that it was called the "model settlement" among those who impartially were able to appraise its achievements and administration.

Shanghai was practically non-existent just a little more than a hundred years ago, when in 1842 Great Britain at the Treaty of Nanking, had the Chinese open this fishing port to foreign trade and obtained the right to open commercial establishments and found a settlement. The British had recognized the importance of this fishing port as a harbour for a hinterland serving at least one hundred eighty million people.

By 1937, the date of the outbreak Sino-Japanese War, this village had become the biggest town in China with six million inhabitants, the fifth largest port in the world, a city that harboured every nationality, a city with skyscrapers and modern factories. All this had been achieved by cooperation between the nations having interest in the China trade, and in spite of everything previously said to the contrary, by the cooperation and the help of the Chinese.

The first British settlement was founded in 1843, in a small area adjoining the Whangpoo River, the life-line of Shanghai. The Whangpoo is a tributary of the Yang-tse, the largest river of China, and navigable for over one thousand six hundred kilometers from the sea, and its business center lies about twenty kilometers from where the Whangpoo flows into the Yang-tse.

The conditions the first British settlers found were rather dismal. The area they were assigned, and in which alone, they were permitted to reside, was itself mostly a marshy swamp surrounded by swamps that bred diseases of all kinds.

A French settlement was founded a few years later, and soon afterwards an American settlement was established.

The International Settlement itself dates from 1845 when the British, French and the United States Consuls drew up a code of regulations applicable to the two concession areas, namely the French and British settlements. In 1863 the United States, which in the meantime obtained a concession area of its own joined the International Settlement, but the French had withdrawn in 1862 and since then governed their concession as a separate unit. A Chinese area, by far the largest part of the city, surrounded the foreign settlements and thus Shanghai consisted of three separate administrations flourished and grew, a growth which was only possible because of all of the cooperation of all countries concerned.

While at the beginning of the International Settlement was a purely Anglo-American affair the accent on the Anglo, all other countries had treaties with China, and that meant nearly all European and many South American Countries, later adhered to the regulation of the Settlement, and directly or indirectly had a say.

The marshy swamps were drained, the canals were filled in to make place for roads and while Shanghai never became a paradise of sanitation, it compared favorably with any city in Asia.

One of the main problems facing the city was to keep the Whangpoo navigable to ocean-going ships. It is too shallow and continuously silted up by the mud brought from the interior by the Yang-tse in such quantities as to even colour the sea a muddy yellow. This herculean task was accomplished by the Whangpoo Conservancy Board, as everything in Shanghai, an international affair composed of the Commissioner of Foreign Affairs for the province of Kiangsu, the Shanghai Commissioner of Customs and the Shanghai Harbor Master, the first one a Chinese, the other two usually foreigners. The success of the work done by this agency reflected itself best in the growth of the port.

The settlement slowly expanded its area, and soon was not inhabited by foreigners, but mostly by Chinese who found the political stability, order, sanitation and freedom it offered, very much to their liking.

The executive power of the International Settlement was vested in the municipal Council consisting since 1926 of five Britains, three Americans, two Japanese and three Chinese. This Council was elected annually. Following the election a "rate-payers" meeting was held at which the early yearly budget was discussed and adopted, and other important decisions taken. This meeting, in a way the parliament of the Settlement, consisted of those who paid "rates", the "rate" being the only tax levied by the city. It was a property tax pure and simple.

Anybody who had property and paid the tax was entitled to a vote. Large property owners disposed of course a large block of votes. The division of nationalities among the councillors was due to a gentleman's agreement and corresponded roughly to the property held by each nationality.

The council was assisted in grave decisions by The Consular Body consisting of the consuls of those Nations considered treaty powers.

It is still wondered at how the International Settlement managed all its affairs with the property tax only, which was by no means heavy, and still was able to have a very efficient police force and fire brigade, keep roads in repair, staff and maintain a health department, several municipal hospitals and schools.

The police force itself was a lesson in international cooperation. It contained a majority of Chinese, many Indians for traffic duty, and foreigners of every nationality. To keep order in a city like Shanghai was no small job, considering its teeming population that changed continuously and did not have to register, and with its alleyways and little Chinese villages, harbouring more people than many a foreign town. Nevertheless, the incidence of crime was never above that expected in a large city and harbour. Apart from the regular police, Shanghai had a "special police" consisting of volunteers who were called upon to do duty in case of an emergency. The International Settlement even had its Army, the "Shanghai Volunteer Corps", entirely made up of volunteers who gave their time and money to make the organization work. The Volunteer Corps had to do duty several times in its history and proved very effective every time, notwithstanding its mixture of nationalities from every corner of the globe.

All this was achieved by the will of the population to keep their city the way they wanted it. The Council was usually composed of men who had made a success of their own affairs and who applied the same principle to governing the city. A handpicked trained staff, paid well and given a great measure of security, achieved wonders in efficiency and in spite of this comparatively high salaries was cheap through just this efficiency.

The International Settlement also achieved fame as a haven for refugees. One of the reproaches usually laid at the door of the Settlement was that it provided a hideout for criminals, fugitives from justice, as well as adventurers. While this was true to a certain extent, what are the few hundred of this category to the more than forty thousand refugees, who with no other place to go to, found a welcome in Shanghai, and were able to build themselves a new life to a certain extent. Of course not the smallest amount of credit for this must go to the Chinese, who, had they really wanted to, could have prevented this influx. On the other hand, Shanghai also provided a place of refuge for many a Chinese political refugee, and humanity in the form of all these refugees owed the former International Settlement a debt of gratitude.

After the war, Shanghai became an integral part of China but it's international spirit and life was well-preserved up to 1949. And today Shanghai despite its skyscrapers and modern factories is slowly returning to what it was, a spot on the map, a living example that cooperation freely arrived at, is still the best guarantee of development.

Paul Hoffmann

13. Paul to Family 2-2-52

Letter written to family by Paul and Shirley when they finally anticipate they will be able to leave Shanghai

February 2nd, 1952 No.66
My dearest ones,
Your letter from the 15th arrived last Monday and so we were without any mail for the last week. I hope tomorrow another letter will arrive. If you have a look in the calendar you will see that today is Saturday and therefore, I am affected today by the "Saturday Blues" – a sickness which only befalls foreigners and strangely enough only in Shanghai. (On Saturdays the list with the exit-visas is published). As you can guess from the above, we have not got our visa again. In fact, it is nonsense that I am so impatient, but if we do not get it until the 16th we cannot reach the ship and that means we must fly, and if we don't get the visa until mid-March, we probably have to wait until after the birth. So, you can see I have all reason to be impatient.

I was as usual quite happy with your letter and I hope that father has started his new job and it is not too exhausting. Mom still should be patient and if she hasn't found a job until we will arrive, I can guarantee her a job as a babysitter with a beautiful baby. Shirley says mom shouldn't write letters with the machine during the time she takes classes, since she'll unlearn again what she already learned.

What you are writing about travelling with a baby is probably true, but we have quite little amusement except making plans and therefore we enjoy it. You can be reassured that with Shirley's and my attitude that nothing will happen that might harm the baby. We will certainly consult a doctor before we go on a trip. Until today I have not received news from Erich and Licci in London. I don't think this is nice. It seems they talk more than act. A lady travels from here to New Zealand and I will send a small gift to Ila even though she doesn't write.

Should we reach the ship our address will be c/o Messagerie Maritime, passenger on SS Felix Roussel and the itinerary is Hong Kong 7th of March, Manila 9-10th of March, Saigon 13-16th of March, Singapore 18th, Colombo 23rd, Djibouti 29th, Suez 2nd of April, Port Said 3rd, and Marseilles 7th of April. From there to Milan to the consulate and we will write you where our address will be.

I have already bought the books for dad. I managed to get them all except one. I will send them directly from Hong Kong, but if we should not be able to leave soon I will try to send them in a different way. Have you already sent the medicines which we ordered a while ago? You have never told the price, how should I encash here? If you haven't sent it yet, don't send it, because if everything goes well the answer to this letter will not reach us here anymore.

Winter has finally started, which means that for 5 days it is raining and snowing and the temperature is between 0 and 5, which of course is the worst weather imaginable. Of course, I go out only very occasionally, as I have nothing to do but my daily walk like a reindeer.

I wrote Teva about the Frigidaire and he will write you whether he wants it or not with the permit. Should we have to fly, we will fly with a line which lands in Israel (Scandinavian Airlines) and interrupt the journey for one week, naturally. Of course, this would be great for Shirley. Many thanks for the advice about the security check, I had no clue about it, but I don't really understand what dad means with *"screening"*. Please write again in detail what I should ask for. Should we travel by ship I'll go to the consulate in Manila. I will not request the papers as

PAUL HOFFMANN

long as we don't have the exit-visa.

Well, again this is everything for now. I hope to receive yours and Praeger's mail tomorrow. Please send the letter as usual to Boston.

With the warmest regards

Your
Paul

Acknowledgements

IN THE LATE spring of 2016, I attended a book talk hosted by the Jewish Historical Society of Greater Hartford at the public library in Avon, Connecticut along with a couple of members of my book club who were, like me, intrigued to hear a local author speak about how her family had fled Norway to escape the Holocaust. At the end of the presentation, Estelle Kafer, then Executive Director of the JHSGH, closed out the evening by saying that the JHSGH had acquired a substantial amount of archival material on the Jewish Community of Greater Hartford and was interested in the stories of Jews who had joined the community from around the world. I approached Estelle to tell her about the stories I had, and she asked me if I knew that the traveling exhibit of the Shanghai Jewish Refugees Museum would be at our Jewish Community Center in West Hartford, Connecticut in November of that year. I told her I had heard of the museum a few years earlier through a *New York Times* article and that the building that housed the museum had been the Ohel Moshe Synagogue, where my parents were married in March of 1950. Estelle was excited to hear of a local connection, and with her help a panel about my father, Paul Hoffmann, who escaped Vienna, Austria to Shanghai in 1938 was included in the exhibit.

Thanks go out to the individuals responsible for turning the wheels that started the process of telling my Dad's story. The pivotal moment that led to this book came shortly before the opening of the exhibit. Estelle contacted me to see if I would be able to host the guest speaker for the opening night of the exhibit, Dr. Liliane Willens, author of *Stateless in Shanghai*. Not only did Liliane's story parallel the lives of both my parents, they had common friends and acquaintances. I showed her the memoir which my father had written for our family, and Liliane immediately told me she thought I had a book. On a subsequent trip to Shanghai, Liliane took a copy of the memoir with her and showed it to her publisher, Graham Earnshaw. I will never forget Liliane's voice over the phone the day after she returned from Shanghai. "Good news! Graham wants to publish your book!" I am forever grateful to Liliane for her initiative, support and friendship that made this book possible.

I am tremendously appreciative to Charlie Olsen for helping me understand how a writer becomes an author. It was his expertise in the field of publishing that gave me the confidence to move forward with this project.

I must thank Sophie Sobkowiak for her terrific work translating many German letters and documents covering over one hundred years of Hoffmann family history. These translations were invaluable in helping to gain greater understanding of so many of the events in the book.

I cannot offer enough thanks to my dear friend, Robin Schwartz, who painstakingly reviewed each chapter with me, not only as another set of eyes on the text, but also helping to ensure that the message of hope and love was always present. Also, many thanks to Mary Louise Stover, whose feedback helped bring the book to completion.

My brother, Abraham Hoffmann, cousins Jackie Mee, Ronald Bernard, Ilana and Neil Plain and Karl Schenker have been a vital resource as they shared stories and photographs that helped support the content included in the book.

I could not have completed this book without the encouragement of my children, David and Cara, and David's wife Erica. My grandchildren Jonathan and Alexis have also been there to remind me to keep going. Cara has been hands on with helping me with the nuances of editing and communicating.

My beloved husband, Doug, spent many months, during a pandemic, while going through chemotherapy, hearing me shout across the hall, "How does this sound?" and helping me through my challenges with technology. Doug loved and admired my father and mother, and he was as eager as I, if not more so, to share their amazing story. My sadness that he passed away before he could see this book in print is countered by the knowledge that he would be so very proud. I could not have done it without him.

Jean Hoffmann Lewanda
April 2021

About The Editor

Jean Hoffmann Lewanda was born in April of 1954 in New York City, one year after Paul and Shulamis Hoffmann arrived in America. She received an undergraduate degree from the University at Albany, her masters degree from New York University, and a Sixth Year Certificate from the University of Connecticut. Jean was a Special Educator for forty years in both private and public schools across all grade levels in the Greater Hartford area in Connecticut. Now retired, Jean lives in Yardley, Pennsylvania near her children and grandchildren. She now shares her family story by participating in Holocaust Education programs.

CPSIA information can be obtained
at www.ICGtesting.com
Printed in the USA
BVHW070815220222
629676BV00005B/14

9 789888 552740